Veronika Eberhart

Garten sprengen

Spector Books

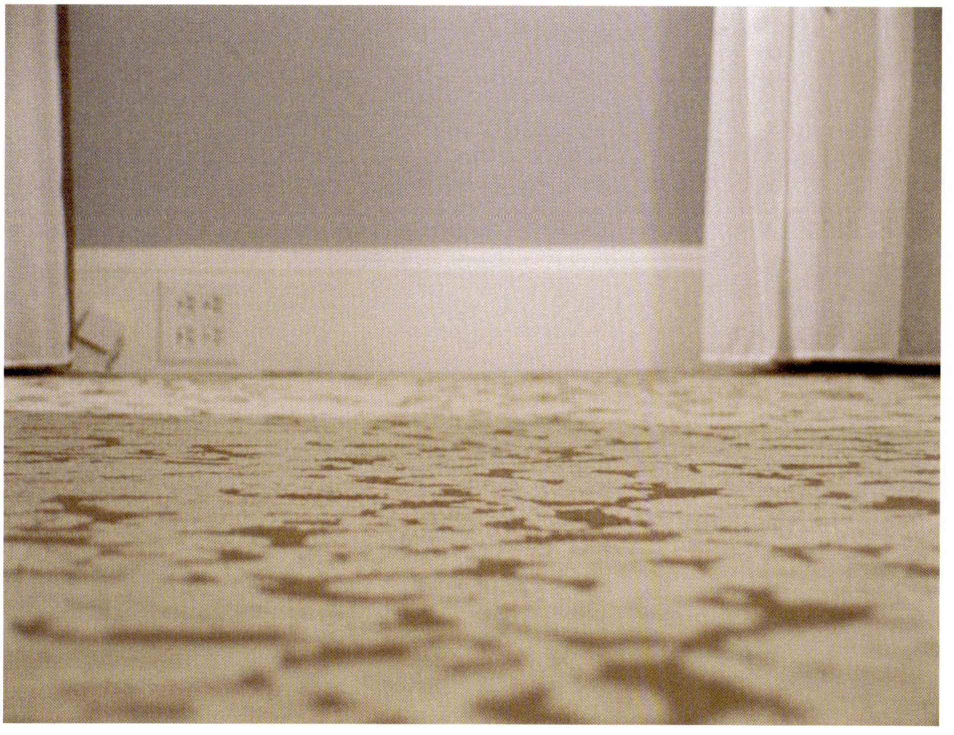

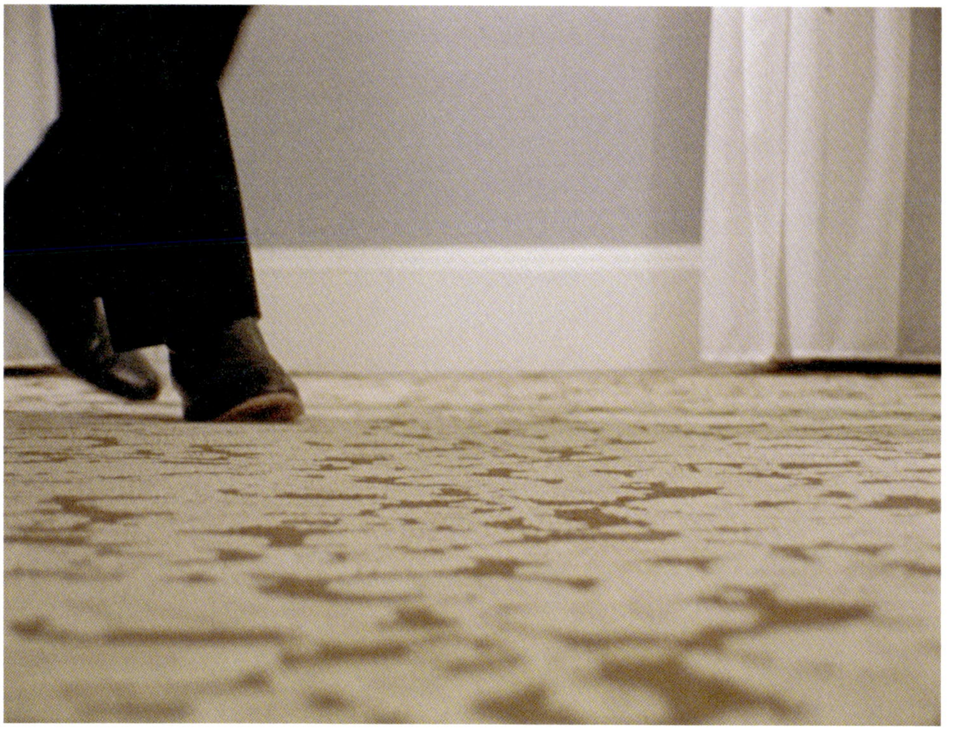

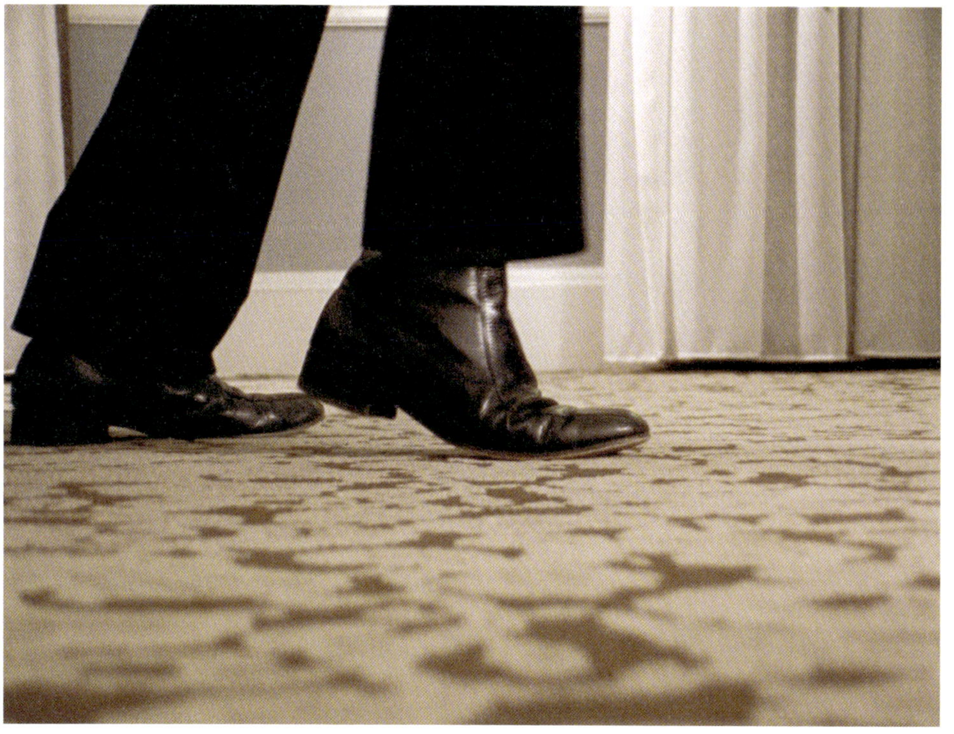

Inhaltsverzeichnis *Table of Contents*

Do you wanna see something? S. 15	*Do you wanna see something?* p. 23	Kevin Vennemann
Timely S. 35	*Timely* p. 43	Veronika Eberhart
	The Blacklist p. 89	Ian F. Svenonius
Die ganze Wüste ist eine Pause S. 101	*The whole desert is a pause* p. 111	Brenda Guesnet
	Ausstellungsansichten *Exhibition views* S. | pp. 49–87	

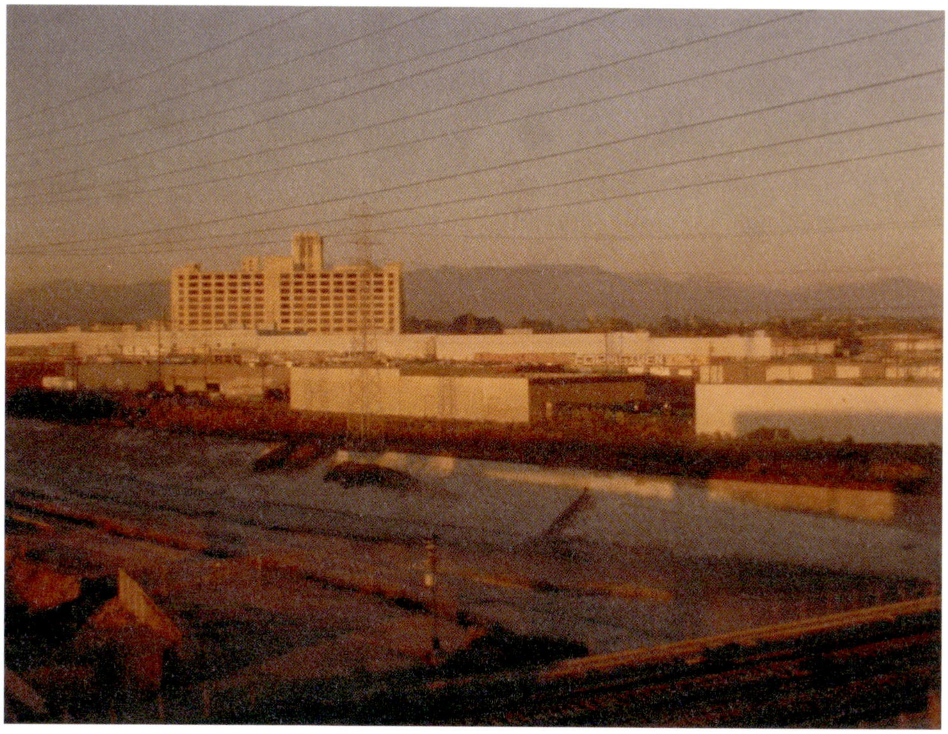

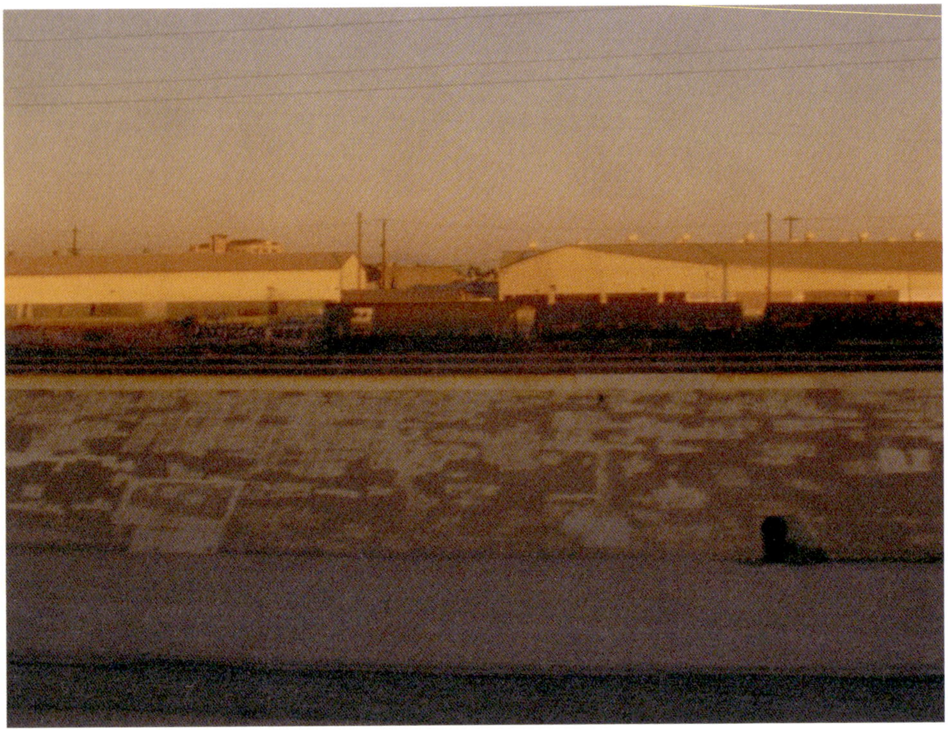

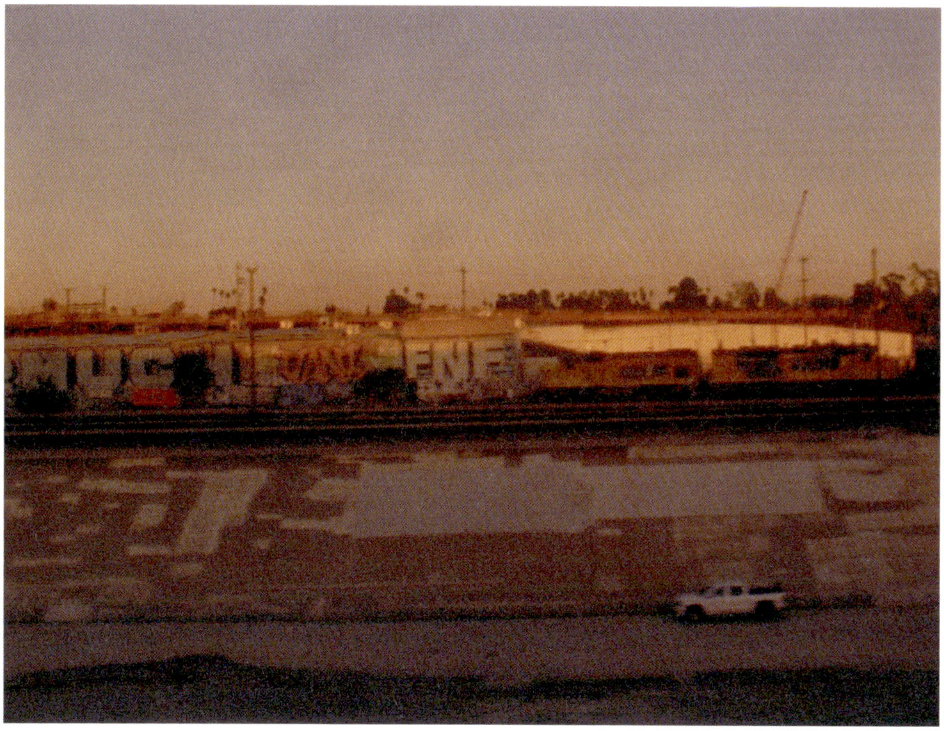

Do you wanna see something?

Kevin Vennemann

1 Northrop Frye, „Archetypical Criticism: Theory of Myths“, in: Frye, *Anatomy of Criticism: Four Essays*, Toronto: University of Toronto Press, 2007, S. 171.

„Hey,
do you wanna see something?“

In einem vor Jahren gedrehten zweitklassigen Action-Thriller kommt es schon im ersten Filmdrittel und lange vor den klärenden Schlägereien und Schießereien zu einem kostbaren Ruhemoment in Los Angeles. Der einsilbige Held begegnet auf seiner Reise zu sich jener hilflosen Frau, die in dieser hartnäckigsten Kinotrope immer schon die Seine war. Er wird sie retten müssen, auch ihr vaterloses Kind. Um herauszufinden, ob sich der Aufwand überhaupt lohnt, muss er wissen: „Hey, do you wanna see something?“ „Yeah“, sind Mutter und Sohn sich einig, dann rauscht der silberne Mustang im kalifornischen Spätnachmittagslicht durch den einbetonierten Los Angeles River, in diesem Sommer trägt er kaum Wasser. Jahre später wird Veronika Eberhart hier am Fluss eine ähnliche Strecke zurücklegen. Für ihren Film *Garten sprengen* (2022) folgt sie im selben Licht demselben halb toten Fluss: Industrieruinen und Strommastenwälder, Verkehr und Lagerhäuser. Die Betonböschung ist mit weiß übermalten, auf diese Weise jedem diskursfähigen öffentlichen Raum entrissenen, Murals und Graffiti übersät.

Im Action-Thriller ist der Held Stuntfahrer von Beruf, er kennt sich mit Autos aus, führt jetzt Tricks vor, die alle begeistern. Endlich zeigt der Sohn durch die Windschutzscheibe auf etwas, von dem er nicht wissen konnte, dass er es hatte sehen wollen: An diesem goldenen Nachmittag, während der Soundtrack den Fahrer als echten Menschen und wirklichen Helden besingt, hält der Mustang vor einem Abschnitt des Betonflussbettes, der vollkommen überwachsen ist mit Kalifornischen Platanen, Wüsten-Beifuß und Pfahlrohr. Mit Kalifornischen Weiß-Eichen und Kalifornischen Stein-Eichen, mit Kalifornischem Buchweizen, Lampenputzergras, Wunderbaum. Mit Wrights Stechapfel, Großer Brennnessel, Johannisbrotbaum, mit Blauem Holunder, Kreuzblättriger Wolfsmilch, Kalifornischem Mohn, mit Strahlenloser Kamille, Kleiner Wasserlinse, Blaugrünem Tabak. Mit Gewöhnlichen Spitzkletten, mit Selbstkletternder Jungfernrebe, mit Toyon, Kalifornischen Küstensonnenblumen, Breitblättrigen Rohrkolben, mit Gold-Johannisbeeren, Amerikanischen Gleditschien, Gewöhnlichem Tellerkraut. Mit Chilenischem Hammerstrauch, Acker-Rettich und Mauer-Gänsefuß. Mit Gewöhnlichem Reiherschnabel, Frischgrünem Zypergras, Quirliger Borstenhirse und Mexikanischen Washingtonpalmen, mit vielem anderem mehr, mit vielen indigenen Pflanzen. Mitten in Los Angeles öffnet sich hier ein gesprengter Garten, eine grüne Welt. So hat der Literaturwissenschaftler Northrop Frye die kurzen Idyllen in vielen Shakespeare-Stücken genannt: momentane Auszeiten, zwar mitten in der „Zivilisation", doch vor ihr verborgen und geschützt.[1] Hier, in diesen wilden Verstecken, kann man zu sich finden, eine neue Perspektive gewinnen, die Welt dort draußen beobachten, mit Distanz ihre strengen Regeln und ihre verwaltete Ordnung verstehen, auch die eigene Position und Funktion in ihr. Nach Luft schnappen kann man hier und kurz bei sich sein, bevor es wieder hinausgeht – gewappnet nun.

So weit ist es noch nicht. Noch hocken hier die drei als Heilige Familie in einem leuchtenden Landschaftsgemälde der niederländischen Renaissance bei ihrer Rast auf der Flucht durchs Leben. Freundliche Insekten schwirren an diesem magischen Ort: mitten in einem nicht mehr existierenden Fluss, eines seit der Ankunft weißer Siedler im 19. Jahrhundert nicht mehr existierendes Los Angeles. Die drei sammeln Blätter, der Fahrer macht vor, wie man Steine auf dem zum Fluss hier angeschwollenen Rinnsal springen lässt, und lässt sich mit einem Blick von der Mutter bestätigen, dass er seinen väterlichen Pflichten in Abwesenheit eines Vaters gerecht wird. „That was good!", flüstert sie dem Helden zu, aus dem einfach kein Wort herauszubekommen ist. Den kleinen Sohn, erschöpft von der Reise in ein anderes Sein, die weiter nicht hätte sein können, trägt er der jungen Frau in die Wohnung und dort ins Bett. Sie ahnen nicht, diese drei, dass das Schlimmste ihnen noch bevorsteht.

•••

Wann immer das Hollywood-Kino in und um Hollywood herum spielt, lässt es seine Held·innen selten aus Los Angeles entkommen. Sie waren hergekommen, jetzt müssen sie es hier schaffen oder auf dem Rückzug zugrunde gehen. Die siedende Sehnsucht dieser Figuren nach einer grünen Welt ist in diesem Kino so präsent wie Hanns Eisler als historische Figur in Veronika Eberharts Film *Garten sprengen:* nicht zu sehen, doch immer drängend, spektral. Zu hören ist, wie Eisler 1947 vor dem Ausschuss für unamerikanische Umtriebe unermüdlich darauf insistiert, dass seine Arbeit in Deutschland seit Jahrzehnten als große Dichtung gelte – als Rückzugsmöglichkeit vor dem und als Kampf gegen das, was auch immer der Kongressabgeordnete John E. Rankin für Poesie halten mag. Anwesend ist in *Garten sprengen* Eisler auch als Komponist jenes eponymen Liedes, das die Sprengung des zivilisatorischen Gartens fordert. Eisler und Brecht jedoch wollen nichts zerstören. Ihre Sprengung kümmert sich um das und gießt, was in Rankins Garten vernichtet wird: Indigenes, Wucherndes, vermeintlich Unvollkommenes, Fremdes. Unkraut. Versengten Rasen. Nackten Boden. Eine grüne Welt.

In *Drive* (Nicolas Winding Refn, 2011) rettet der Held mit seinem silbernen Mustang seine neue Familie gleich zweimal – am Ende des Films rettet er ihr das Leben und zu Beginn befreit er sie aus einer in Los Angeles wirklich bedrohlichen Lage: Das Auto der beiden hat einen Motorschaden, von nun an fährt er sie herum. Seit jeher wird das Hollywood-Kino von Männerheroen wie dem mysteriösen Fahrer als Erlöser ausgelieferter Frauenfiguren dominiert. Lou Eisler ist in Brentwood eine Ausnahme-Heldin: Damit Hanns im Alltag überleben kann, kümmert sich Lou um Haus und Hof und Garten, dient als Sekretärin, setzt Briefe auf, fährt ihn herum, weil er keinen Führerschein hat und haben will. Mag sein, dass sie die Gärtnerforderungen nach Geld für Pflanzendünger nur aus Pflichtbewusstsein an ihren Vermieter weiterleitet, sich tatsächlich nicht allzu sehr daran stören würde, wenn auch der Garten rund um 162 South Burlingame Avenue sich in eine grüne Welt verwandelte. Mag sein, dass sie uns *diesen* Garten dann zeigen wollen würde.

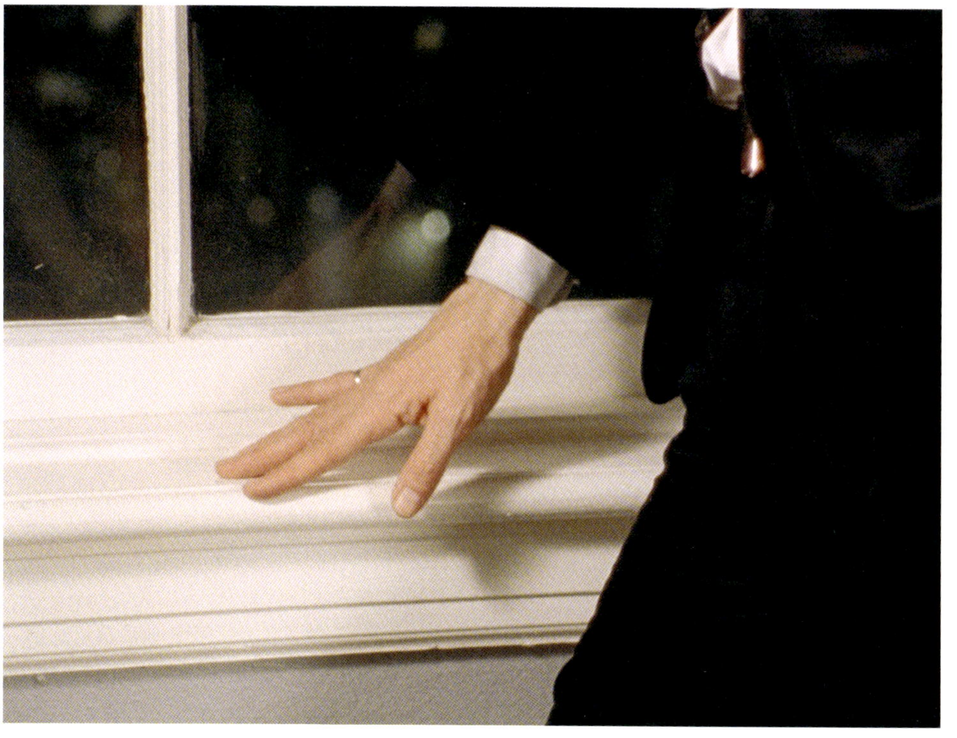

Do you wanna see something?

Kevin Vennemann

1 Northrop Frye, "Archetypical Criticism: Theory of Myths," in: Frye, *Anatomy of Criticism: Four Essays*, Toronto: University of Toronto Press, 2007, p. 171.

"Hey,
do you want to see something?"

About a third of the way into a recent second-rate action thriller, long before the brawls and shootouts at the end, there comes a precious moment of calm in Los Angeles. While on his journey, the monosyllabic hero meets the very damsel in distress who, according to this most persistent of cinematic tropes, has always been "his woman." In order to find out if saving her and her fatherless child is worth the effort, he needs to know: "Hey, do you want to see something?" Both mother and son do want to see something, and then – in the late afternoon California light – the silver Mustang roars over the concrete bed of the Los Angeles River, carrying very little water that summer. Years later, in this same light, Veronika Eberhart's film *Garten sprengen* (2022) covers a similar distance: industrial ruins and forests of electricity poles, traffic and warehouses line the half-dead river. On the concrete riverbanks, scores of murals and graffiti have been whitewashed and are thus removed from public discourse.

Back in the action thriller, the hero is a stunt driver by profession; and so, knowing a thing or two about cars, he performs exciting tricks for the boy. Finally, the boy points through the windshield to something he couldn't have known he wanted to see: on this golden afternoon, as the soundtrack extols the driver as a real person and a real hero, the Mustang stops in front of a section of the concrete riverbed that is overgrown entirely with Californian Sycamores, California Mugwort and Giant Reed. Coast Live Oaks and Valley Oaks, Californian Buckwheat, Fountain Grass, Castor Bean. Sacred Datura, Dwarf Nettle, Carob. With Blue Elderberry, Spotted Spurge, California Poppy, Pineappleweed, Common Duckweed, Indian Tobacco. Rough Cocklebur, Virginia Creeper, Toyon, California Brittlebush, Broadleaf Cattail, Golden Currant, Honey Locust, and Miner's Lettuce. Chilean Sea Fig, Wild Radish, and Nettle-leaved Goosefoot. Common Stork's Bill, Tall Flatsedge, Carolina Bristlemallow and Mexican Fan Palms. There are many more plants, many of them indigenous, too. Here, in the middle of Los Angeles, a *gesprengter Garten* opens up in the double sense of the German verb: it has been thoroughly irrigated and it looks as if it has exploded.

A Green World. This is what the literary scholar Northrop Frye called the brief idyllic moments in many of Shakespeare's plays: momentary time-outs located at the center of "civilization" but hidden and protected from it.[1] Here, in these wild hiding places, there is space for self-discovery. You can gain a new perspective here, observe the world out there and, from a distance, understand its strict rules and prescribed order, including your own position in it. You can gasp for air here, rest and regain your strength, and be alone for a moment before venturing out once more.

For now, the three of them are still sitting here – similar to the Holy Family in the center of a luminous Dutch Renaissance landscape painting – while resting on their flight through life. Friendly insects are buzzing in this magical place: in the middle of a defunct river; it's a Los Angeles that has not existed since the arrival of white settlers in the 19th century. The Holy Family collects leaves, the driver demonstrates how to make stones skip on the trickle that has swollen now to the size of a proper river. With a sideways glance he makes sure that the mother is aware of him fulfilling his paternal duties in the absence of the boy's father. "That was good!" the woman whispers as he carries the boy, who is exhausted from this long journey into another state of being, as the driver takes him into the young woman's apartment and to bed. Little do they know, these three, that the worst is yet to come.

•••

Whenever Hollywood cinema is set in and around Hollywood, it rarely allows its heroes to escape Los Angeles alive. They have come here, now they must make it here. The simmering longing of these characters for a Green World is as present in Hollywood cinema as Hanns Eisler is as a historical character in Veronika Eberhart's *Garten sprengen:* not to be seen, but spectral. In 1947, before the House Un-American Activities Committee, Eisler could be heard insisting tirelessly that his work had been regarded as great poetry in Germany for decades – as a retreat from and against whatever Representative John E. Rankin might consider poetry.

In the film, he is also present as the composer of the song calling for the *Sprengen* of the garden of civilization. Eisler and Bertolt Brecht's *Sprengen*, however, does not intend to destroy anything. Instead, it takes care of and waters whatever is quashed in Rankin's garden: anything indigenous and straggling, anything supposedly imperfect, foreign. Weed. Scorched lawn. Bare ground. A Green World.

With his silver Mustang, the mysterious hero in *Drive* (Nicolas Winding Refn, 2011), saves his new family twice. First, he rescues them from a situation that is more threatening in Los Angeles than anywhere else: the woman's car has broken down, and from now on, he drives them around. At the end of the film, he literally saves their lives. Hollywood cinema has always been dominated by this driver and other masculine saviors of helpless women. In Brentwood in 1942, Lou Eisler is the exceptional heroine: For Hanns to survive in everyday life, Lou takes care of both house and garden, she serves as his secretary, she writes letters, and drives him around because he doesn't have a driver's license and doesn't want one. It might be her sense of duty that makes her ask the landlord for money for plant fertilizer, while, in fact, she wouldn't mind too much at all if the garden around 162 South Burlingame Avenue turned into a Green World as well. Maybe she would even show us *this* garden.

LOU EISLER
162 SOUTH BURLINGAME AVE
BRENTWOOD PARK
LOS ANGELES, CAL.

DECEMBER 8, 1942.

DEAR DR. CARR :

I EXPECTED YOU LAST WEEK ON THURSDAY AND FRIDAY AND ALSO TO DAY, AS WE HAVE TO SPEEK ABOUT IMPORTANT THINGS. I FOUND A VERY NICE HOUSE IN BEVERLY HILLS, WHICH MAKES IT POSSIBLE FOR MR. EISLER TO WORK IN HIS STUDIO IN SPITE OF THE GASOLINE SITUATION. MOREOVER THE HOUSE IS DOUBLE AS LARGE FOR HALF THE PRIZE, BUT THE MEAN THING IS THAT MY HUSBAND HAS THE CHANCE TO COMMUTE FROM THERE. I WOULD LIKE TO MOVE ON JANUARY 1. PLEASE WRITE ME OR LET ME KNOW, WHEN YOU LIKE TO DISGUSS THINGS WITH ME.

THE GARDENER TOLD ME THAT HE HAS TO FURTILIZE THE GARDEN THIS WEEK AND PUT SOME PLANTFOOD ON THE GROUDS, OTHERWISE THE GARDEN WILL GO TO PIECES. HE THINGS THAT PLANTFOOD WILL COST ABOUT $ 2. PLEASE TELL ME WHAT TO DO, I ALSO HAVE TO PAY HIM FOR THIS MONTH.

YOURS SINCERLY

LOU EISLER

DECEMBER 2?,1942

LOU EILSER
162 SO BURLINGAME

DEAR DR. CARR :

I JUST RECEIVED YOUR LETTER OF DECEMBER 18. IT SEEMS THAT YOU DID NO NOT UNDERSTAND MY LETTER OF DECEMBER 15. AS YOU DONT ANSWER ANY OF I MY QUESTIONS. I WOULD LIKE VERY MUCH TO COME TO A FRIENDLY UNDERSTANDING WITH YOU AND CERTAINLY I DONT WANT TO MOVE OUT HERE BEFORE YOU OR THE REAL ESTATE AGENT DID NOT CHECK UP HERE. BUT I SHOULD LIKE TO HAVE A DECISION FROM YOU AS QUICKLY AS POSSIBLE AS I HAVE TO MAKE MY OWN ARRANGEMENTS WITH AN OTHER HOUSE WHICH I DID NOT DUE YET AS I WAS WAITING FOR YOUR ANSWER. MISS DOUGAN TOLD ME THAT YOU ARE COMMING OUT HERE ON WEDNESDAY,THAT WOULD BE VERY NICE,AS WE COUKD TALK OVER THINGS MUCH EASIER.CERTAINLY YOU W WILL GET THE RENT DUE TO YOU,BUT FIRST WE HAVE TO DISCUSS THE CONDITIONS. (RENT FOR DECEMBER IS ALREADY PAID AND THE RENT FOR XXX JANUARY IS NOT DUE UNTIL JANUARY FIRST. I CAN NOT ACCEPT YOUR DATE OF DECEMBER 23. BEFORE THINGS ARE NOT SETTLED AS I DONT INTEND TO STAY HERE IN FEBRUARY UNDER THE PRESENT CONDITIONS.

THE GARDENER TOLD ME THAT THE $2 ARE ONLY COVERING FURTILIZATIONS AND PLANT FOOD FOR THE FLOWER BEDS.BXXXXXX FURTILIZARION OF THE GROUNDS WOULD COST AN OTHER 5-7$. BUT THE THING TO DO IS MAYBEE THAT YOU TALK OVER THIS THINGS WITH HIM. HE FEELS THAT FURTILIZATIONS HAS TO BE DONE NOW. HIS PHONE IS : 50779 S.M. IF YOU RATHER LIKE ME TO TELL HIM WHAT TO DO YOU HAVE TO TELL ME ON WEDNESDAY,IF YOU ARE COMMING.

PLEASE LET ME KNOW FOR SURE WHEN YOU INTEND TO COME (OTHERWISE I MIGHT BE AWAY) I HAVE TO BRING MY HUSBAND AVERY D/ TO HOLLYWOOD NOW) IF YOU DONT COME LET ME KNOW YOUR DECISIONS

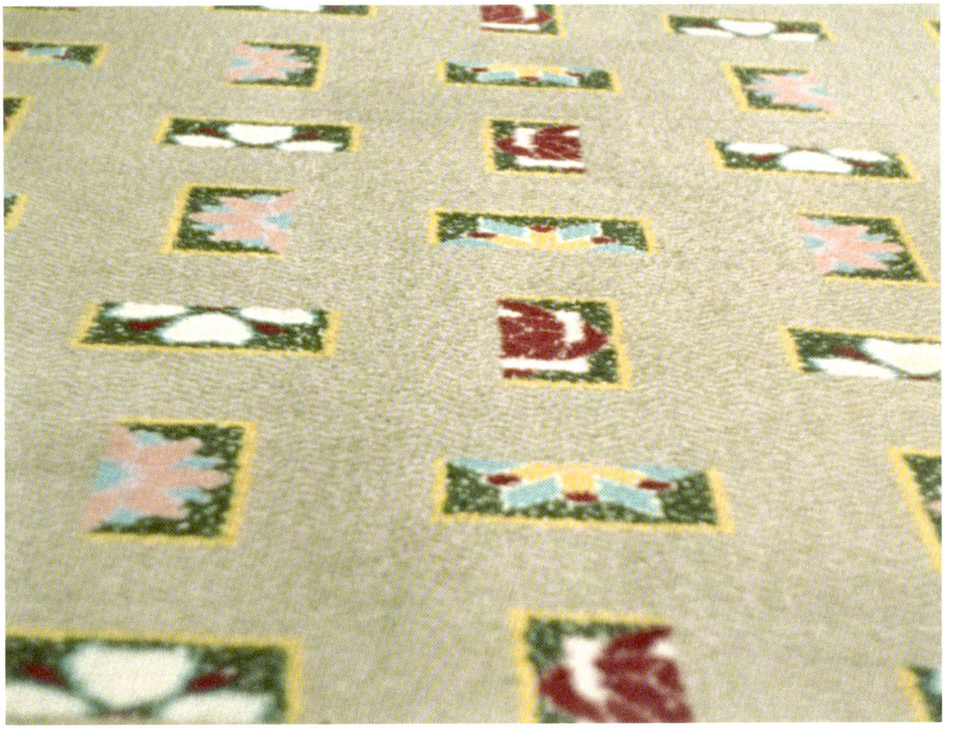

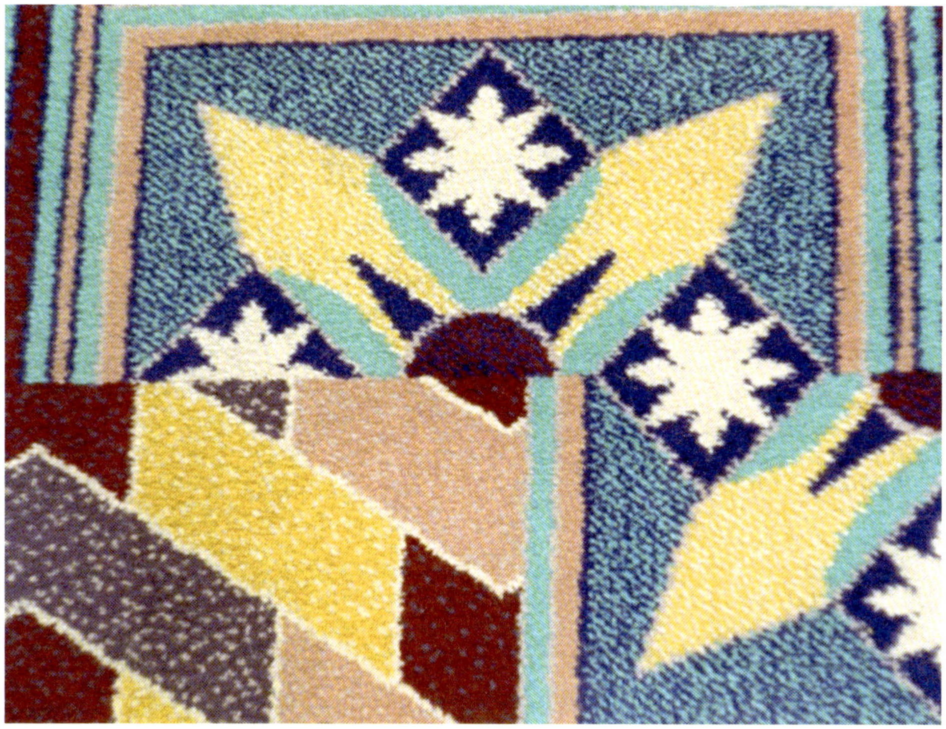

Timely

Veronika Eberhart

1 Salt 'N' Pepa, *Tramp*, Remix 12" Single, New York: Next Plateau Records, 1987. Gloria Lynne, *I'm Glad There Is You*, Bayside: Everest Records, 1960.

2 Allan Sutton und Kurt Nauck, *Documentation of American Record Companies and Producers 1988–1950*, Denver: Mainspring Press, 2018, S. 499.

3 Die erste Fassung wurde 1929 anlässlich des zehnjährigen Bestehens der Kommunistischen Internationale (Komintern), der Zusammenschluss kommunistischer Parteien zu einer weltweiten gemeinsamen Organisation, verfasst. Die „Komintern" fand ab 1931 weite Verbreitung und wurde ins Russische, Polnische, Französische, Englische, Spanische und in andere Sprachen übersetzt. Vgl. Pierre Crépon, *The Wire playlist: Hanns Eisler fighting songs*, https://www.thewire.co.uk/audio/tracks/wire-playlist-hanns-eisler-fighting-songs-from-1930s-shellac-to-1970s-free-jazz

4 Bertolt Brecht, Maurice Sugar und V.J. Jerome schrieben die Texte. Mitwirkend unter anderem der Arbeiter·innen-Chor „The New Singers" unter der Leitung von Lan Adomián, die Baritone Mordecai Bauman und Felix Groveman sowie abwechselnd Marc Blitzstein und Eisler selbst am Klavier.

5 *New Masses*, February 25, 1936, Volume 18, No. 9, veröffentlicht von the New Masses, 31 East 27th Street, New York City.

6 ebd.

7 ebd.

8 Moyra Davey, *Burn the Diaries*, New York: Dancing Foxes Press, 2014, S. 28.

9 Allan Sutton und Kurt Nauck, *Documentation of American Record Companies and Producers 1988–1950*, Denver: Mainspring Press, 2018, S. 499.

10 *Hearings Regarding Hanns Eisler: Hearings by United States Congress House Committee Un-American Activities*, Washington: United States Government Printing Office, 1947, S. 40.

11 Hanns Eisler, *Gespräche mit Hans Bunge, Fragen Sie mehr über Brecht*, München: Rogner & Bernhard, 1976, S. 95.

12 ebd., S. 182.

Ein zwanzigminütiger Spaziergang durch Manhattan, New York

führte mich im vergangenen Jahr nach einem Besuch des Rough Trade Stores im Rockefeller Center, Midtown zur Adresse 235 Fifth Avenue, dem ehemaligen Standort von Timely Recording Company. Unter dem linken Arm zwei soeben erworbene Vinylschallplatten[1] blicke ich durch die Fensterscheibe des kurzlebigen und heute nicht mehr existierenden Plattenlabels. Dunkelbraune Holzvertäfelung. Ein Stiegenaufgang mit gewölbtem Geländer, rotbraun verfliester Boden, drei Spiegel als Balken an der Wand. Hinter dem Portierpult sitzt eine Person. Heute befindet sich hier eine Bank.

In Allan Suttons und Kurt Naucks Enzyklopädie amerikanischer Plattenfirmen wird Timely als ein „eher zwielichtiges Unternehmen, über das nur spärliche Unterlagen existieren“[2], beschrieben. Das New Yorker Label brachte zwischen 1935 und 1940 antifaschistische und prokommunistische Schellackplatten in kleinen Auflagen heraus. Darunter auch die Lieder „In Praise of Learning“, die Hymne der Komintern,[3] „Rise Up“, „United Front“ und „The Soup Song“. Bis auf letzteres, dessen Melodie von „My Bonnie Lies Over the Ocean“ stammt, wurden alle von Hanns Eisler komponiert.[4] Zum Zeitpunkt der Veröffentlichung 1936 berichtet die marxistische Zeitschrift *New Masses* über die Wirkung der Musik auf ihre Hörer·innen: „I have seen listeners, time after time, fidgeting in their chairs, infected by the rousing rhythms of the music and almost unable to restrain themselves from breaking into chorus.“[5] Mir geht es nicht viel anders, seit jeher hat Eislers Musik einen mitreißenden Effekt auf mich. Wohl nicht zuletzt deshalb habe ich mich auf die Spuren seines amerikanischen Exils begeben. Das noch recht junge Medium der Schallplatte galt in den 1930er Jahren als Hoffnungsträger der amerikanischen Arbeiter·innenbewegung: „The phonograph came into existence just sixty years ago. By the October Revolution Lenin was using it to spread his personal force into corners where he himself was unable to go. By the time Hitler took over Germany there were hundreds of Hanns Eisler records to feed the Nazi bonfires. But in America records had no direct function in the labor movement until this very year.“[6] Das sollte sich ändern und die Verbreitung solidarischer Lieder im öffentlichen und privaten Raum wurde im *New Masses* Artikel weiter propagiert: „They will be played in homes, to a few men. They will be played at mass meetings where they will stir thousands. In mining towns where men have forgotten how to sing. In shacks by the waterfront. In farmhouses through the West. And every where they will come now, at last at their living form.“[7]

In ihrem essay *Burn the Diaries* schreibt Moyra Davey über die prägende Wirkung eines Plattencovers von Roxy Music (1972) und die damit verbundenen Erinnerungen an eine Jugendfreundschaft.[8] Das Bild auf dem Umschlag ist für sie emotional untrennbar mit dem musikalischen Inhalt verbunden. Umgekehrt erweckt ein Cover die Neugierde manchmal so stark in mir, dass ich einen Kauf tätige, ohne die Musik vorher gehört zu haben. Selten aber habe ich so aufwendig gestaltete Etiketten wie auf den Schellacks von Timely Recording gesehen. Die Optik ist im Comic-Stil gehalten. Zu jedem Song gibt es eine politische Karikatur auf dem Label:
Eine gezeichnete Figur in einem Overall, mit einem Kapperl auf dem Kopf, schwenkt eine Fahne, auf der die Aufforderung „RISE UP" zu lesen ist. Wie ein Banner oder eine Verkündung auf einer Schriftrolle schlängelt sich die Botschaft entlang des Labels. Umgeben von konzentrischen Kreisen, steht die Arbeiterfigur auf einem kartografierten Planeten. Die Erde. Am Horizont erscheint eine Menschenmasse unter den Sternen. Die Hände erhoben, die Blicke erwartungsvoll. Alles scheint in Bewegung zu sein, wie die Platte selbst, sobald sie auf dem Plattenspieler liegt und sich dreht. Am meisten fasziniert mich der ambivalente Gesichtsausdruck der Figur im Vordergrund. Der Mund leicht geöffnet, vielleicht singend, blicken die Augen uneindeutig auf das, was da kommen mag. Überrascht, zuversichtlich oder doch erschrocken?

Auf der anderen Seite der 10-inch wird das Etikett durch den Schriftzug „IN PRAISE OF LEARNING" geteilt. Im oberen Halbkreis ist eine Zeichnung von Phil Wolfe zu sehen, die mehrere Personen in verschiedenen Kontexten beim Lesen und Lernen zeigt. Im unteren Teil eine Aufzählung aller an der Produktion Beteiligten. Verspielt und doch wie eingegossen, macht uns der Schriftzug darauf aufmerksam, wie viele Personen zur Veröffentlichung eines Liedes nötig sind. Liner Notes erzählen immer auch vom kollektiven Moment und dem sozialen Aspekt einer Musikproduktion. Und doch gibt es auch jene Momente, die fast nie aufgelistet sind, wie Lou Eislers Ambitionen, die sie in New York zurückließ, um ihren Mann als Chauffeurin, Sekretärin und Haushälterin in Hollywood zu unterstützen. Ihr Plan, einen Roman über die Emanzipation zweier Schwestern zu schreiben, die Bankiers werden wollten, blieb unverwirklicht.

Die Lieder „The Soup Song" und „United Front" erscheinen mit je einer Zeichnung des Malers und Grafikers Russell Limbach. Im Stil kommunistischer Agitation visualisiert er Situationen antifaschistischer Handlungen, wie die Abwehr eines Messers und das Recht auf regelmäßige Mahlzeiten. Im August 1938 wurde Timely Recording vom House Un-American Activities Committee (HUAC) als eine von 640 Organisationen genannt, die angeblich kommunistisch waren oder auf verschiedene Weise mit der kommunistischen Bewegung zusammenarbeiteten.[9]

So wird auch Eisler in seinem HUAC-Verhör zum Refrain des auf Timely erschienenen Liedes „In Praise of Learning" von Robert E. Stripling wiederholt gefragt: „What do you mean, ‚you must be ready to take over'?" Bevor Eisler seine Erklärung zur Herkunft des Textes, ein Roman von Maxim Gorki, beenden kann, hakt der Vorsitzende nach: „Would it also apply here to the United States?" Und Chief Investigator Robert E. Stripling fährt fort: „It was shown in the United States. He wrote the music for it in the United States."

„No; I wrote the music in 1929 or 1930 in Berlin. It was produced in Copenhagen, in New York – I guess in Paris. It was a theater play", entgegnet Eisler.[10]

Die Wirrungen darüber, ob ein Musik- oder ein Theaterstück an ein bestimmtes geografisches Moment gebunden ist, oder ob es sich nur an eine örtlich begrenzte Öffentlichkeit richten kann, verdichten sich auch angesichts der Tatsache, dass Eisler für Text und Musik verantwortlich gemacht wurde. Später, in den Gesprächen mit Hans Bunge über Brecht, amüsiert sich Eisler über diesen Umstand und erklärt stolz:

> *Sie lasen mir also aus meinen Werken von den Übersetzern angefertigte Übersetzungen vor und behaupteten, das wäre von mir. Na ja, ich kann doch nicht sagen: ‚Entschuldigen Sie, ich bin nur Komponist.' Das ist ja ein läppisches Verhalten. Das ist ja unmöglich. Folglich habe ich diese Texte dann verteidigt als mein Werk.* […] *Es war einer der erfolgreichsten literarischen Diebstähle, die man überhaupt begehen kann. Der Brecht, der ja selbst, wie Sie wissen – weil er sich ein paar Zeilen wo ausgeliehen hat von einer Villonübersetzung –, auf dem Gebiet ein Kenner ist, sagte, das war eine Virtuosenleistung. Dagegen wäre er ein reiner Anfänger. Er hätte es nur mit zwanzig Zeilen gemacht, ich hätte das mit ganzen Opussen von Brecht gemacht. Er war darüber aber sehr gerührt. Er hat mir das wirklich nicht vergessen, obwohl es keine Leistung war.*[11]

Draußen auf der Fifth Avenue hupen vorbeifahrende Taxis, Rhythmen aus den Autoradios verdichten sich mit Wortfetzen von vorbeigehenden Passant·innen. Ich spaziere weiter, diesmal ohne genaues Ziel, und muss an Chantal Akermans Film *News from Home* (1976) denken. An die hypnotische Art, wie sie gesprochenen Text mit der Soundkulisse New Yorks verwebt. An die Momente, in denen ihre Stimme von den Geräuschen der Stadt verschlungen wird. An die Pausen zwischen dem Gesagten und an die Erwartung auf das Wiedereinsetzen der gesprochenen Erzählung. Der Klang ihrer Stimme, der sich teilweise in der Umgebung aufzulösen scheint, erweckt etwas Melancholisches in mir. Dagegen wirkt Eisler in seinen Ausführungen über die *Dummheit in der Musik* fast heiter. Wenn sein belehrender Tonfall in mir widerhallt, kann ich nicht anders, als zu schmunzeln und doch blitzt da eine Hoffnung auf, die im Hören liegt:

> *Die Musik ist eine archaische Angelegenheit. Sie kennen das Wort ‚archaisch'. Es stammt nicht von mir, es stammt von Jung, dem Psychoanalytiker aus der Schweiz. Das Ohr ist zurückgeblieben. Schauen Sie, das Auge, die Intelligenz sind ja mitgeschritten – wenigstens in den sozialistischen Ländern. Aber in den kapitalistischen Ländern ist das Ohr zurückgeblieben. Das Ohr ist einfach etwas Archaisches, Dumpfes. Es ist nicht mitgekommen. Es ist irgendwie noch ein Rückblick, eine Erinnerung an den Zustand der alten Kollektive vor Hunderten von Jahren.* […] *Aber gerade weil das Ohr zurückgeblieben ist, kann es eine gewisse Humanität noch weiterreichen in unsere Zeit.*[12]

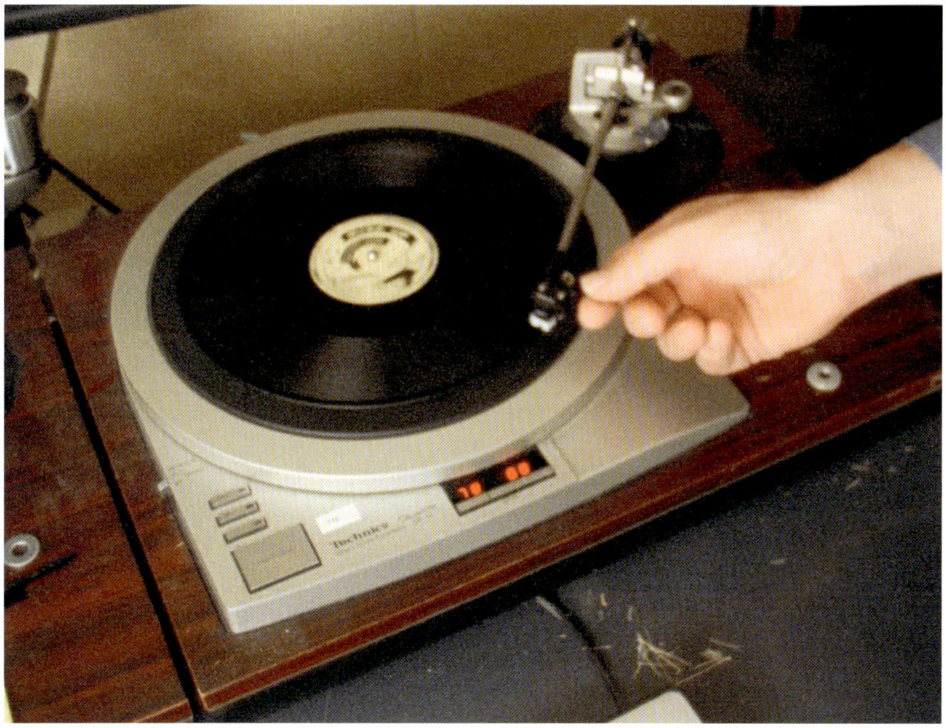
Technics

Timely

Veronika Eberhart

1 *Tramp*, Salt 'N' Pepa, Remix 12" Single, New York: Next Plateau Records, 1987, and *I'm Glad There Is You*, Gloria Lynne, Bayside: Everest Records, 1960.

2 Allan Sutton and Kurt Nauck, *Documentation of American Record Companies and Producers 1988–1950*, Denver: Mainspring Press, 2018, p. 499.

3 The first version was written in 1929 for the tenth anniversary of the Communist International (Comintern), the merging of communist parties into a worldwide organization. The "Comintern" was widely distributed from 1931 and was translated into Russian, Polish, French, English, Spanish, and other languages. See too Pierre Crépon, "The Wire playlist: Hanns Eisler fighting songs," https://www.thewire.co.uk/audio/tracks/wire-playlist-hanns-eisler-fighting-songs-from-1930s-shellac-to-1970s-free-jazz

4 Bertolt Brecht, Maurice Sugar and V.J. Jerome wrote the texts. Performers included the workers' choir The New Singers under the direction of Lan Adomián, the baritones Mordecai Bauman and Felix Groveman, as well as Marc Blitzstein alternating with Eisler himself on the piano.

5 *New Masses*, February 25, 1936, Volume 18, No. 9, published by the New Masses, New York City.

6 Ibid.

7 Ibid.

8 Moyra Daevy, *Burn the Diaries*, New York: Dancing Foxes Press, 2014, p. 28.

9 Allan Sutton and Kurt Nauck, *Documentation of American Record Companies and Producers 1988–1950*, Denver: Mainspring Press, 2018, p. 499.

10 *Hearings Regarding Hanns Eisler: Hearings by United States Congress House Committee Un-American Activities*, Washington: United States Government Printing Office, 1947, p. 40.

11 *Brecht, Music and Culture. Hanns Eisler in Conversations with Hans Bunge*, edited and translated by Sabine Berendse and Paul Clements, London: Bloomsbury, 2014, p. 82.

12 Ibid., p. 166.

Last year,
after a visit to the Rough Trade store
at Rockefeller Center in midtown Manhattan, a twenty-minute walk downtown led me to 235 Fifth Avenue, the former location of the short-lived Timely Recording Company. With two newly purchased vinyl records[1] under my arm, I looked through the window. Wood paneling in dark brown. A staircase with an angled banister, floor tiled in terracotta, three mirrors on the far wall, facing the street. A doorman sitting behind a desk. These days, there is a bank there.

In Allan Sutton's and Kurt Nauck's Encyclopedia of American Record Labels & Companies, Timely is described as a "rather shadowy company for which only sparse documentation exists."[2] Between 1935 and 1940, the New York label released anti-fascist and pro-communist shellacs in small runs. Among these were the songs "In Praise of Learning," the Comintern's anthem "Rise Up,"[3] "United Front," and "The Soup Song." Aside from the last-mentioned song, whose melody derives from "My Bonnie Lies over the Ocean," all were composed by Hanns Eisler.[4] In 1936, the Marxist magazine *New Masses* reported on the music's effect on its listeners: "I have seen listeners, time after time, fidgeting in their chairs, infected by the rousing rhythms of the music and almost unable to restrain themselves from breaking into chorus."[5] For me it's not much different; Eisler's music has always had a mesmerizing effect on me. It's probably one of the reasons why I followed the trail of his American exile.

In the 1930s, the phonograph record was still a very new medium and it was considered a beacon of hope for the American workers' movement: "The phonograph came into existence just sixty years ago," the *New Masses* article continued. "By the October Revolution Lenin was using it to spread his personal force into corners where he himself was unable to go. By the time Hitler took over Germany there were hundreds of Hanns Eisler records to feed the Nazi bonfires. But in America records had no direct function in the labor movement until this very year."[6] This was to change, and the spread of songs of solidarity in public and private space was further propagated in the *New Masses* article: "They will be played in homes, to a few men. They will be played at mass meetings where they will stir thousands. In mining towns where men have forgotten how to sing. In shacks by the waterfront. In farmhouses through the West. And everywhere they will come now, at last at their living form."[7]

In her essay *Burn the Diaries*, Moyra Davey writes about the formative impact of the first Roxy Music's LP cover (1972) and her associated memories of a teenage friendship.[8] For Davey, the image on the cover is emotionally inextricable from its musical content. Indeed, a cover can sometimes spark such a strong curiosity in me that I will purchase the record without having heard the music. Though I've rarely seen such meticulously designed labels as those on the shellacs of Timely Recording. The images are in a comic style. For every song there's a political caricature on the label: A figure in overalls and cap waves a flag upon which the call "RISE UP" can be read. Like a banner or an announcement on a scroll, the message winds along the label. Surrounded by concentric circles, the worker figure stands atop a mapped planet Earth. On the horizon, a mass of people appears beneath the stars. Hands raised, gazes full of expectation. Everything appears to be in motion, like the record itself once it's been laid on the record player and begins to turn. What fascinates me most is the ambivalent facial expression of the figure in the foreground. Mouth slightly opened, perhaps singing, eyes looking vaguely towards that which might come. Surprised, confident, or afraid perhaps?

On the other side of the 10-inch, the label is bisected by lettering that reads "IN PRAISE OF LEARNING." In the upper semi-circle, there is a drawing by Phil Wolfe that shows many people reading and learning in various contexts. In the lower part is a list of all those involved in the production. While the lettering is playful, it's made to look as though it's been poured in, making us aware of just how many people are required to release a song. Liner notes usually recount a collective moment and the social aspect of a musical production. And yet there are also details that are never included – like Lou Eisler's ambitions, which she left in New York in order to support her husband as his driver, secretary and homemaker in Hollywood. Her plan to write a novel about the emancipation of two sisters who wanted to become bankers went unrealized.

"The Soup Song" and "United Front" each came out with a drawing by the painter and graphic designer Russell Limbach. In the style of communist agitprop, he visualized scenarios of anti-fascist action, like fending off a knife or claiming the right to regular meals. In August 1938, Timely Recording was named by the House Un-American Activities Committee (HUAC) as one of 640 organizations that were supposedly communist or in various ways working with the communist movement.[9]

So it was that, during his HUAC interrogation about the chorus of the song "In Praise of Learning," released by Timely, Eisler was also asked again and again: "What do you mean, 'you must be ready to take over'?" Before Eisler can finish his explanation as to the origin of the text, a novel by Maxim Gorki, the chairman presses on: "Would it also apply here to the United States?" And Robert E. Stripling the chief investigator continues: "It was shown in the United States. He wrote the music for it in the United States."

"No; I wrote the music in 1929 or 1930 in Berlin. It was produced in Copenhagen, in New York – I guess in Paris. It was a theater play," Eisler retorts.[10]

The confusion around whether a piece of music or theater is to be linked to a specific geographical situation, or whether it can only be directed towards a localized public also came to a head as Eisler was deemed responsible for both text and music. Later, in the conversations with Hans Bunge about Brecht, Eisler could laugh about the situation, proudly explaining:

> *HUAC had had the words to my songs translated; they read them out and attributed them to me. Now well, I couldn't very well say, 'I'm sorry, but I'm just a composer'; such a political position is indecent. It's impossible. I therefore decided to defend those texts as if they were my own.* […] *That's how I appropriated to myself the best of Brecht's plays, one of the most successful literary thefts of all time. Brecht, himself an expert in this field – you remember that, somewhere, he borrowed a few lines from a Villon translation – told me that mine was a virtuoso performance and that, compared to me, he was a mere beginner: he had only taken twenty lines, but I had appropriated entire works by him. He was very touched by it all and never forgot what I did for him although it could hardly be called an accomplishment.*[11]

Outside, on Fifth Avenue, passing taxis honk their horns, rhythms from car radios are compressed with scraps of conversations by passersby. I continue walking, this time without any particular aim, and I think about Chantal Akerman's 1976 film *News from Home*. About the hypnotic way she weaves spoken text into New York's soundscape. About the moments when her voice is swallowed up by the noise of the city. About the pauses in her speech and about the anticipation for the spoken narrative to resume. The sound of her voice, which sometimes seems to dissolve into the surroundings, evokes something melancholic in me. In contrast, Eisler seems almost cheerful in his remarks on the *Stupidity in Music*. When his lecturing tone resonates in me, I can only smile, and yet there's this flash of hope, which lies in the act of listening:

> *Music is an 'archaic' thing (Carl Jung's word, not mine). The development of the ear lags behind the other senses. The eye and the intelligence have progressed, at least in the socialist countries, but in the capitalist countries the ear lags behind. It's archaic, numb. It's lethargic and lazy, it hasn't kept up. It's somehow a backward look at the old collectives of hundreds of years ago.* […] *But precisely because the ear is retarded, it's able to bring a certain humanity into our time.*[12]

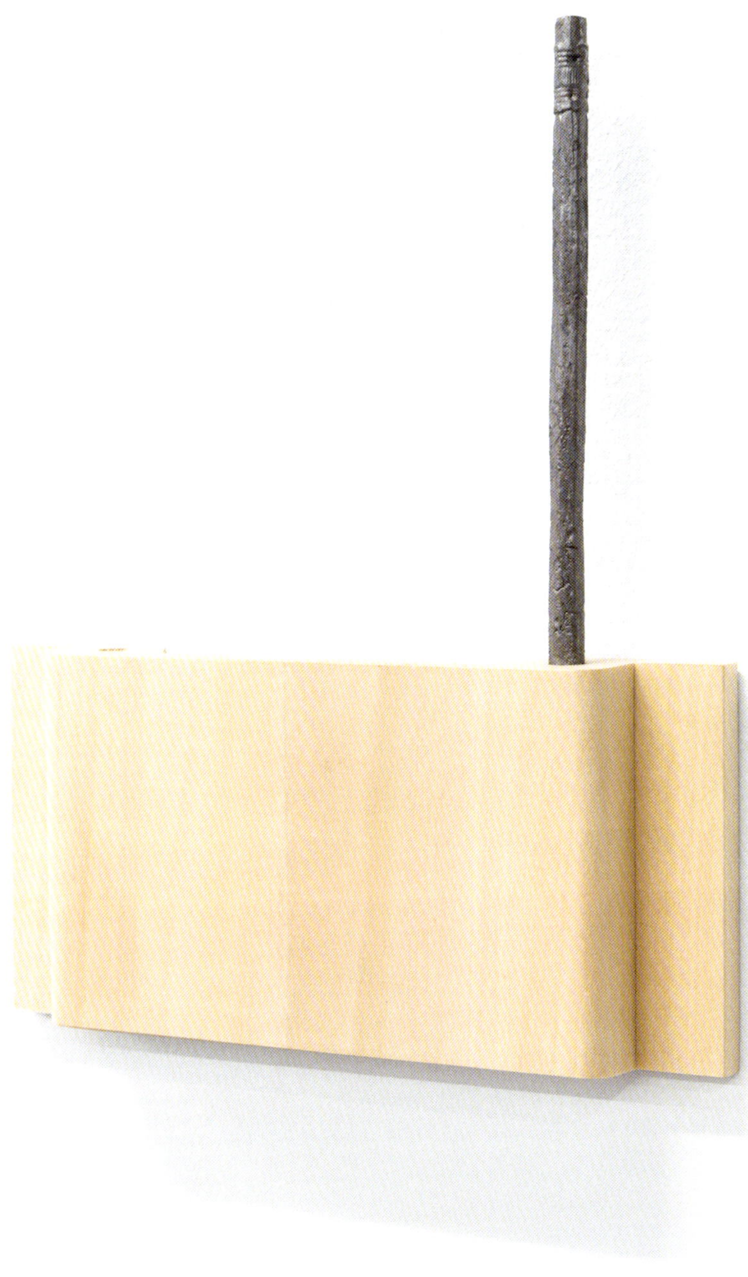

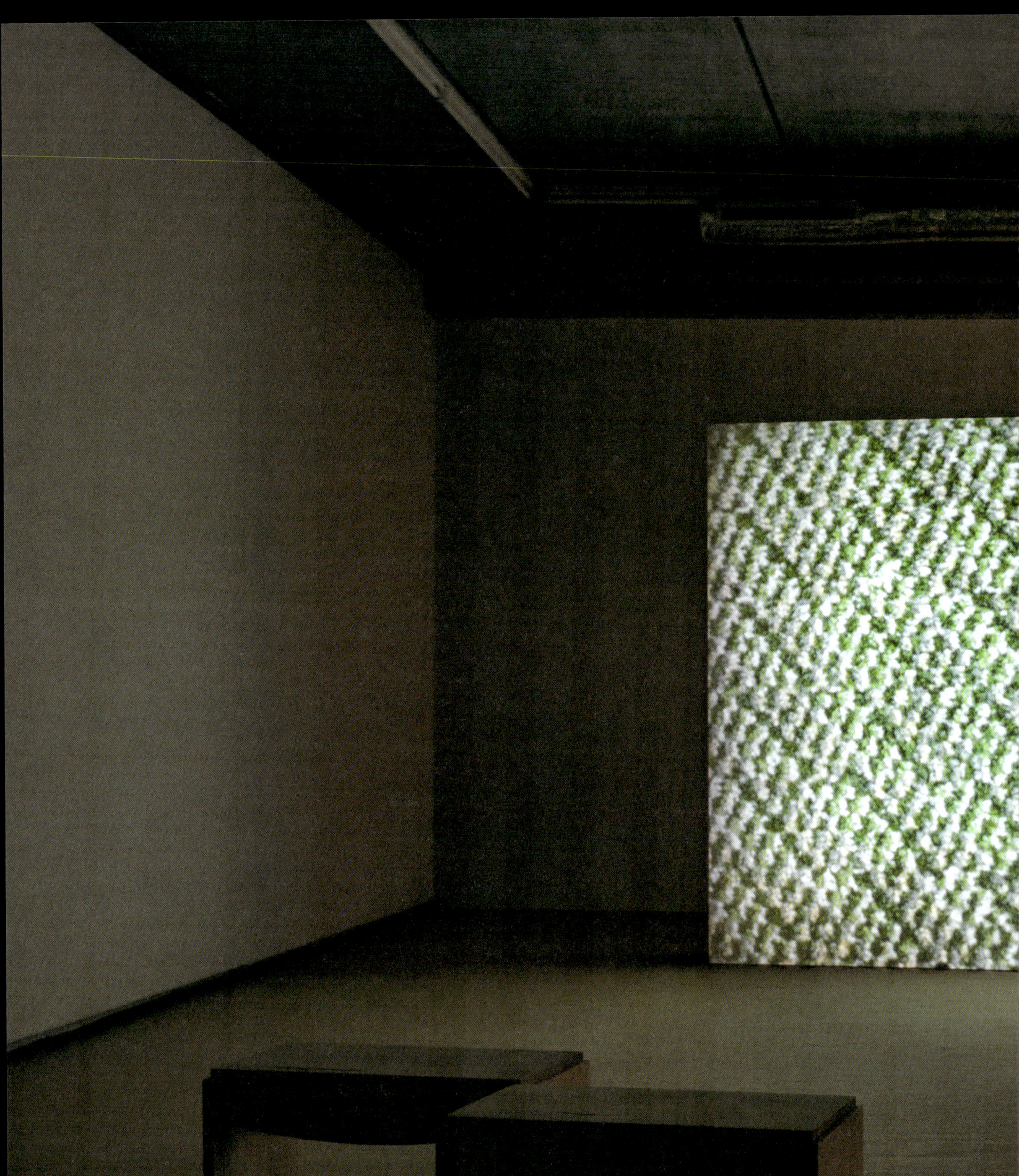

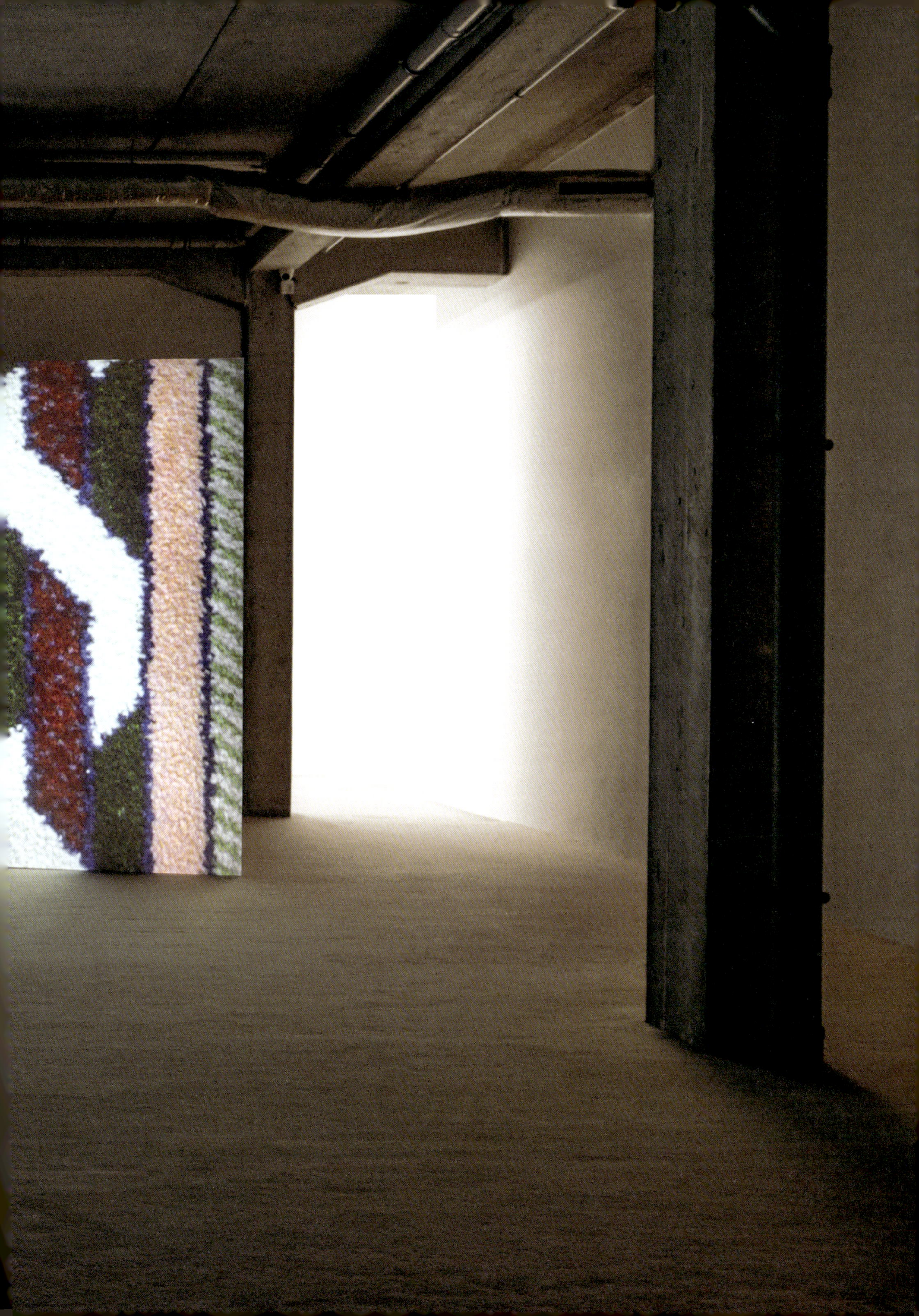

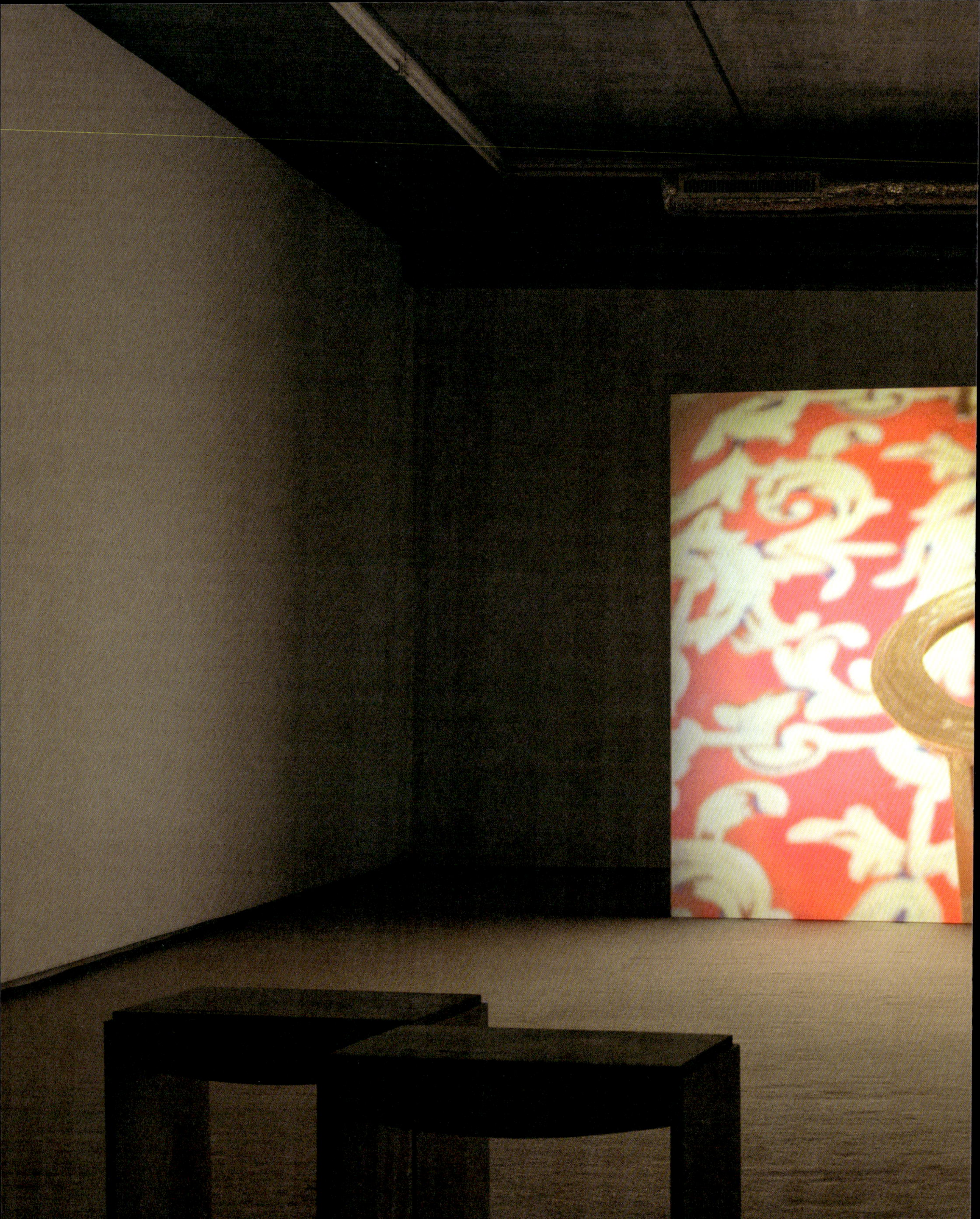

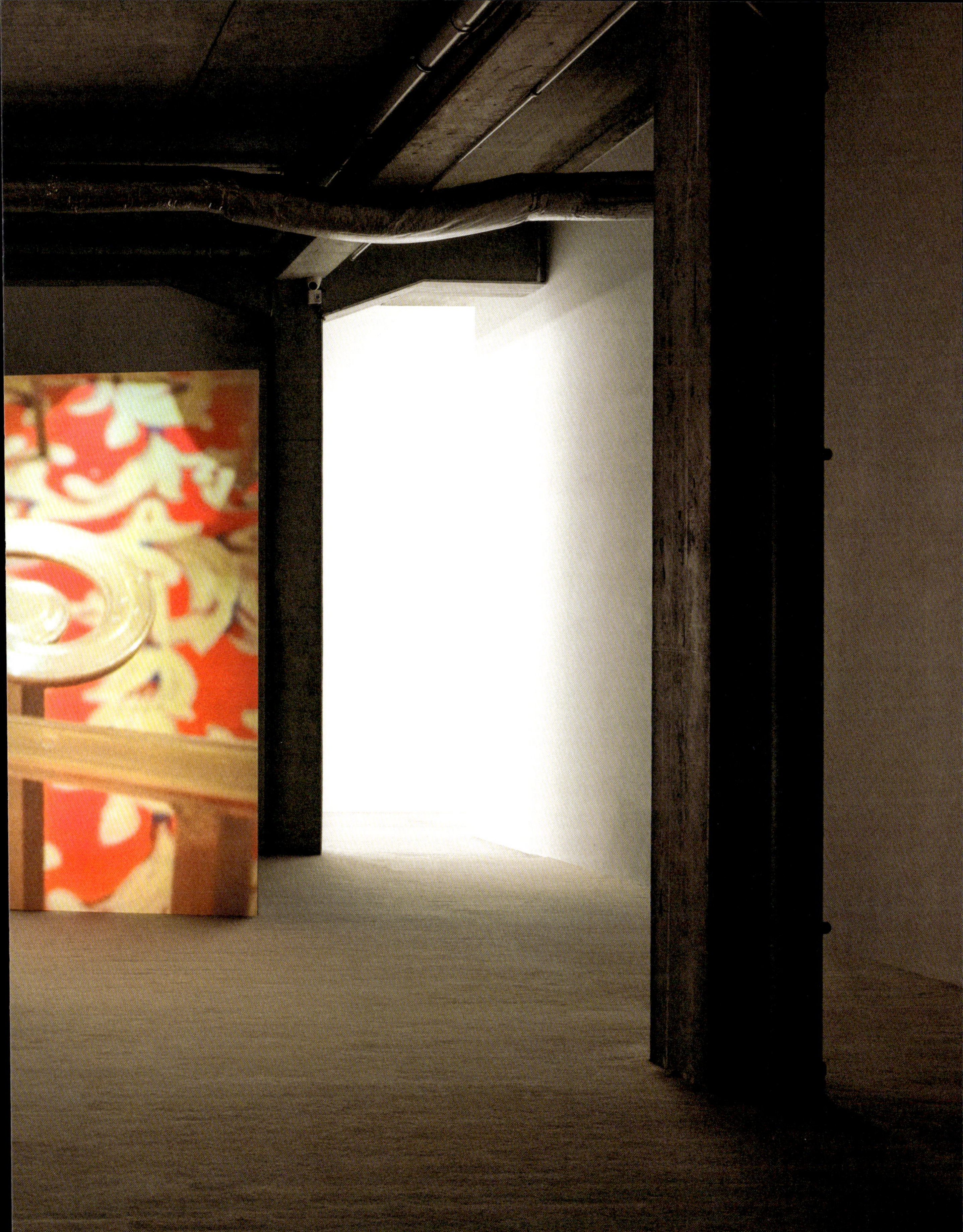

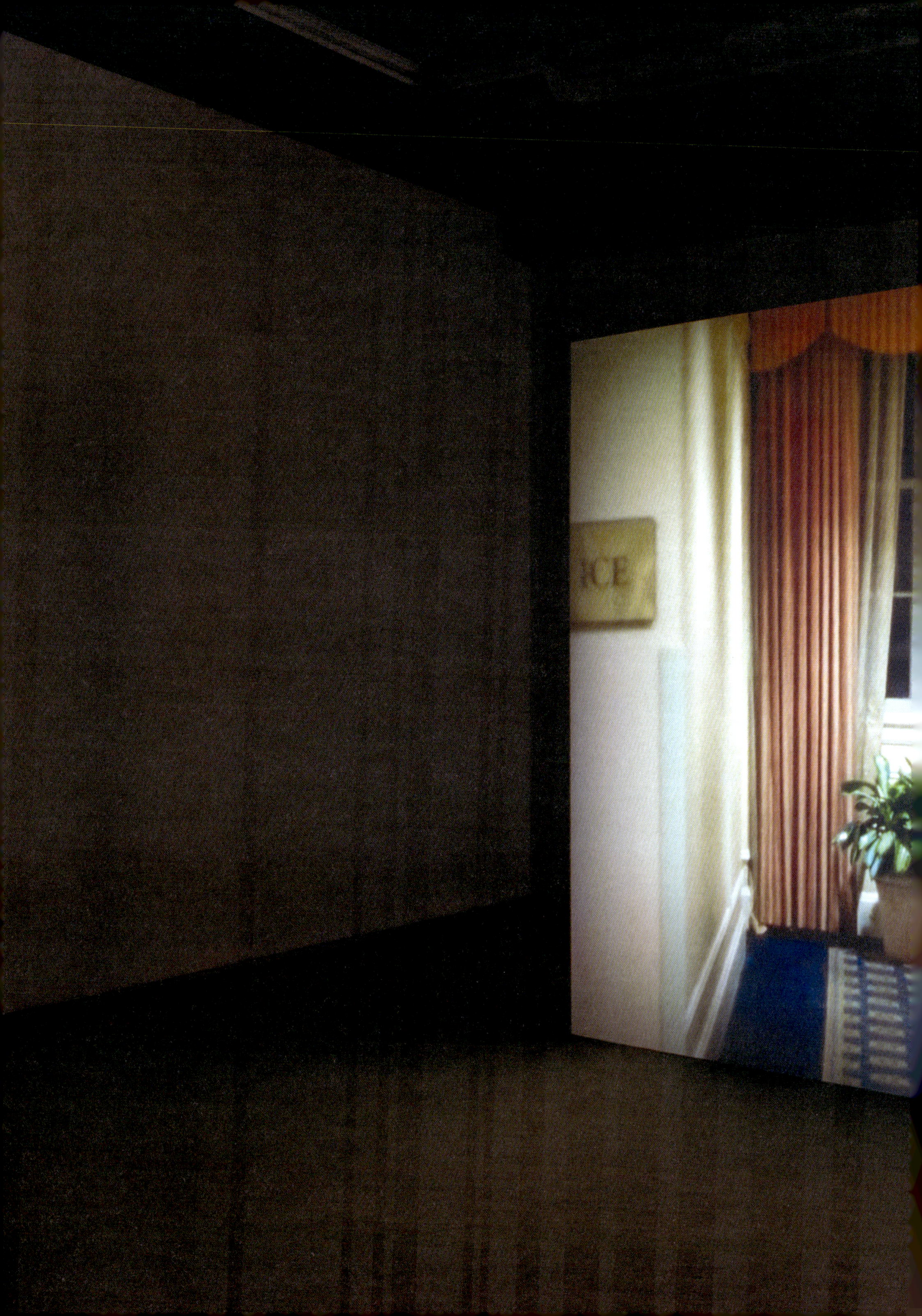

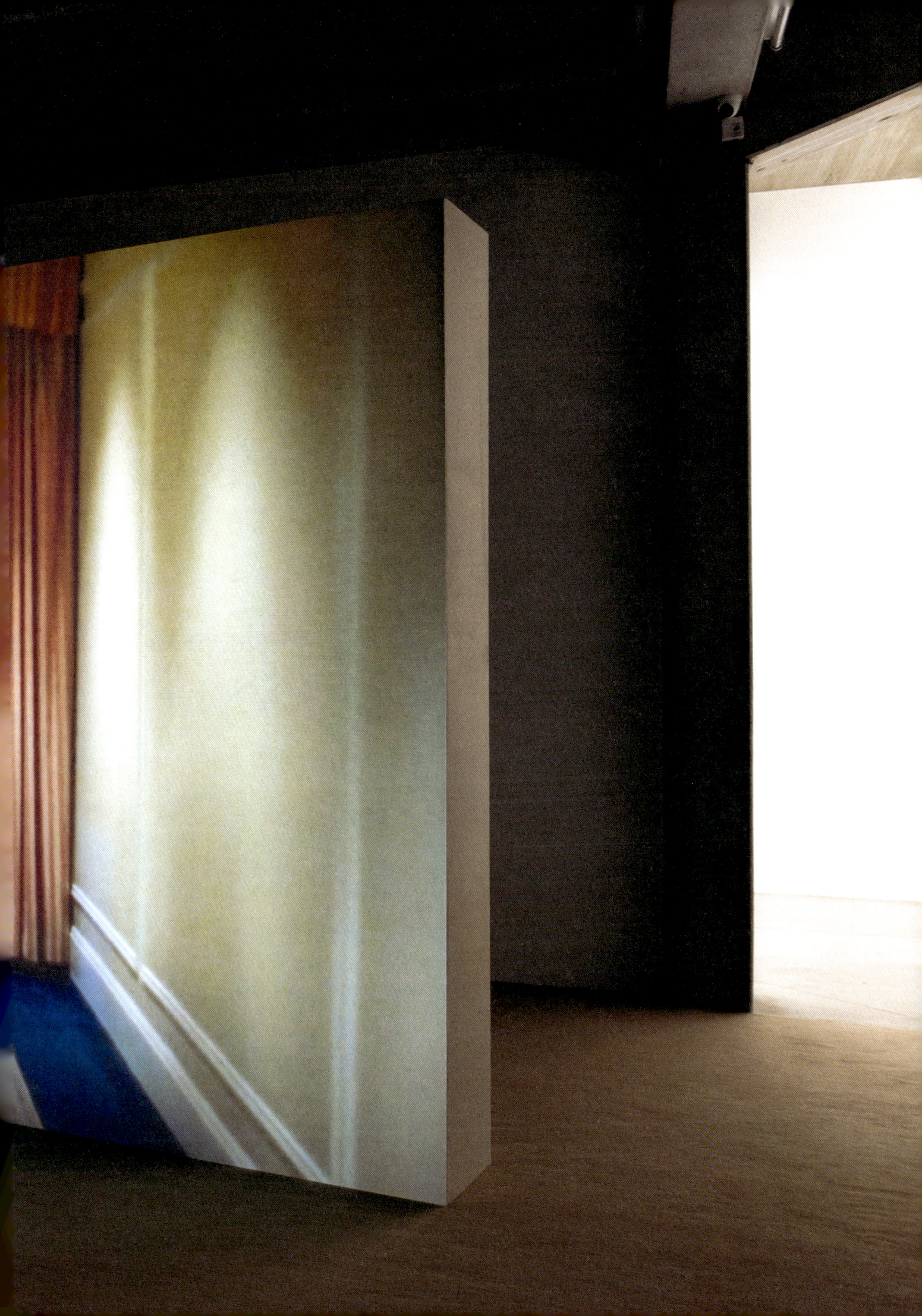

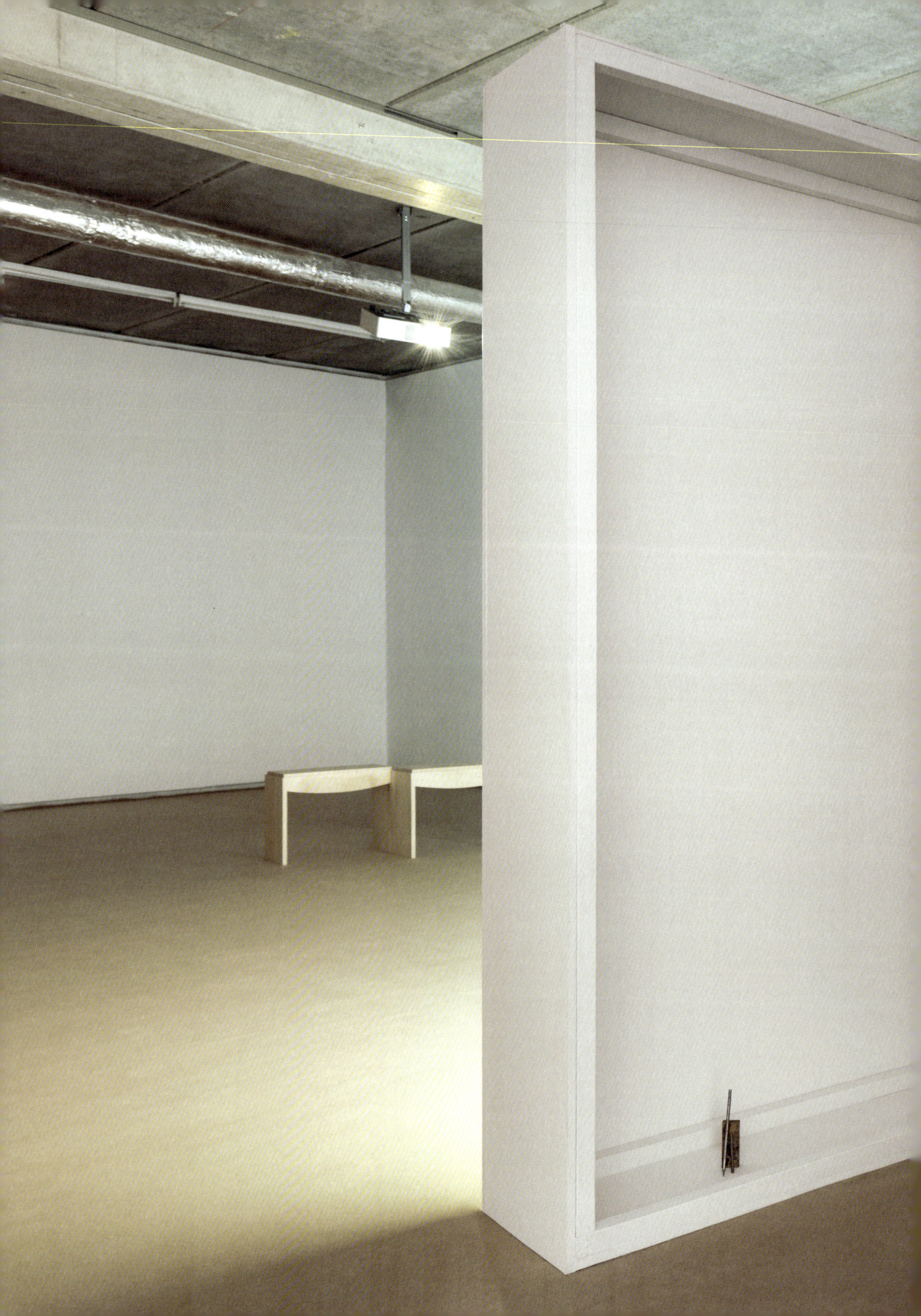

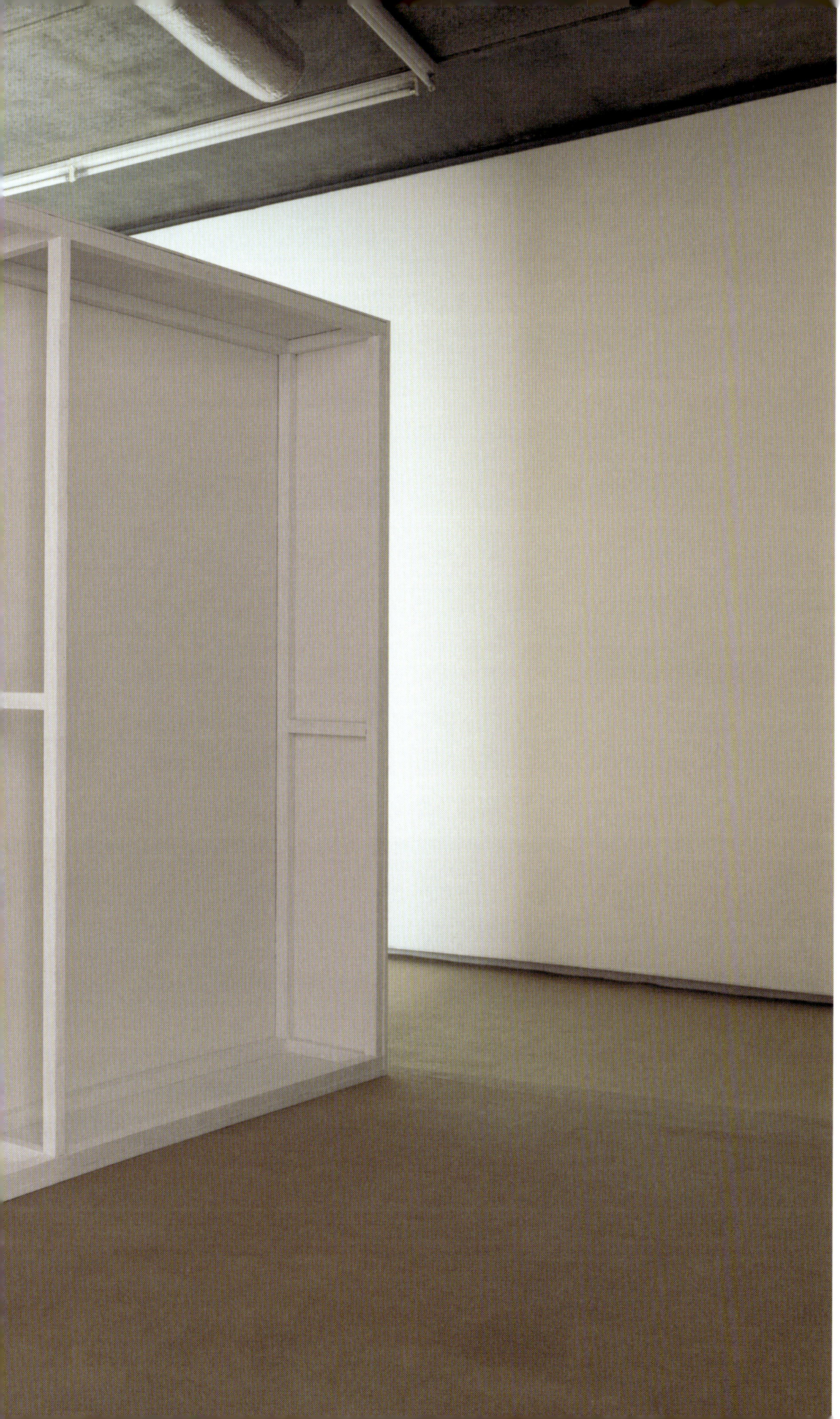

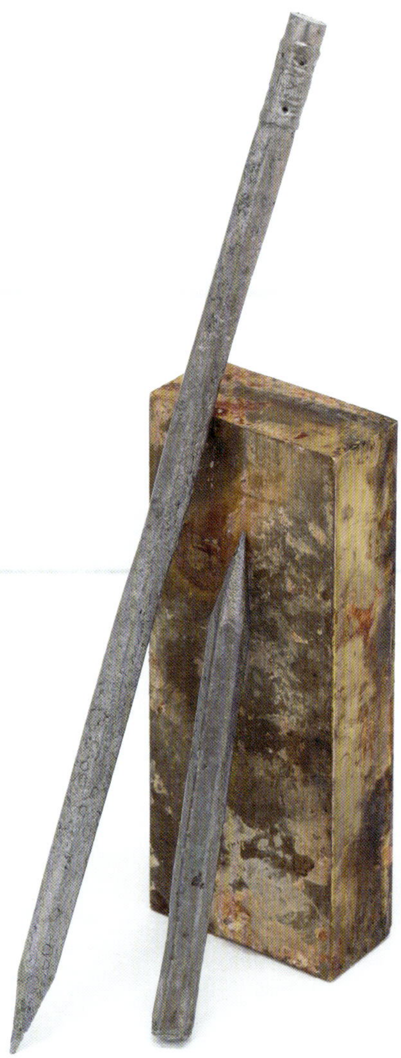

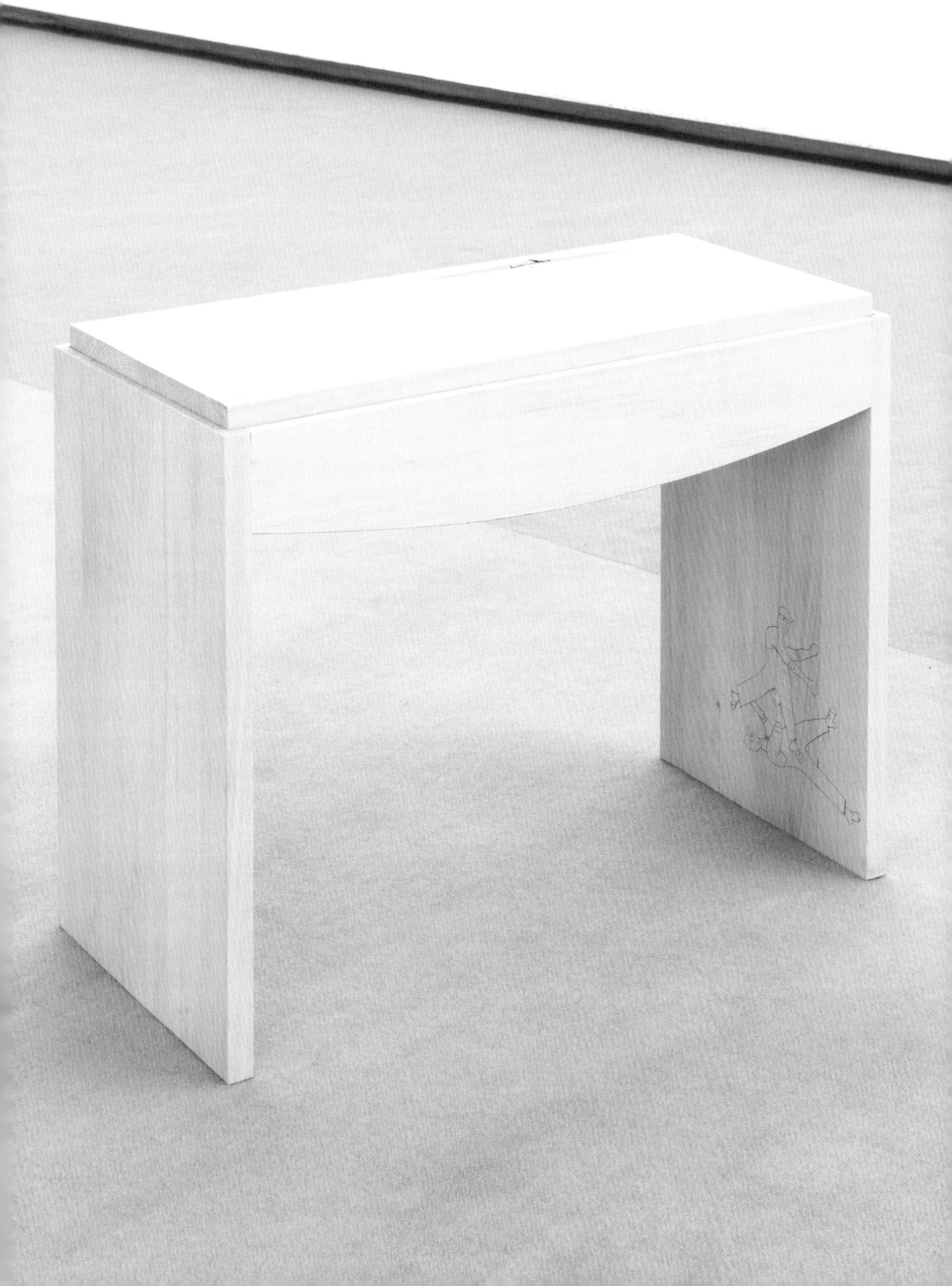

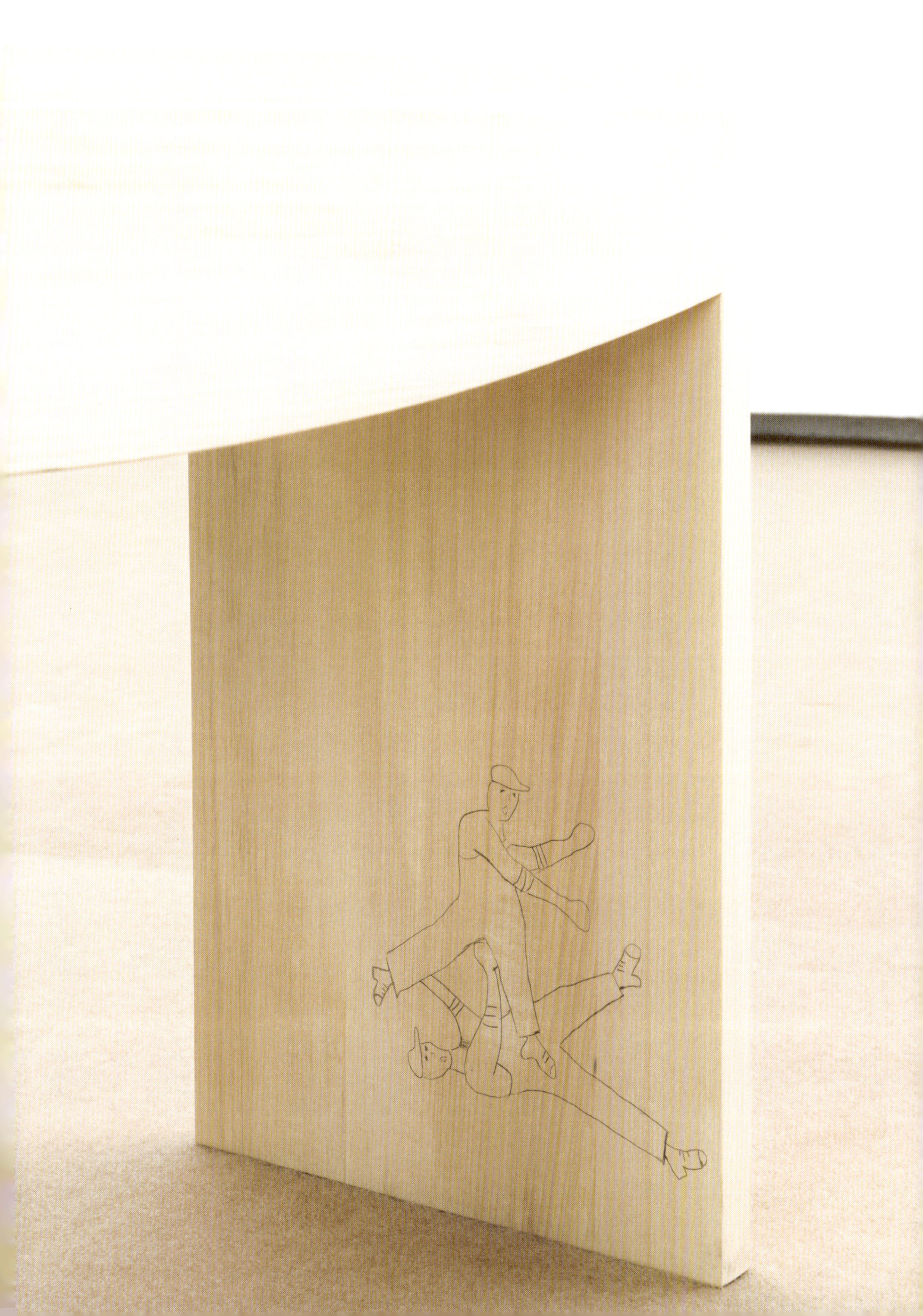

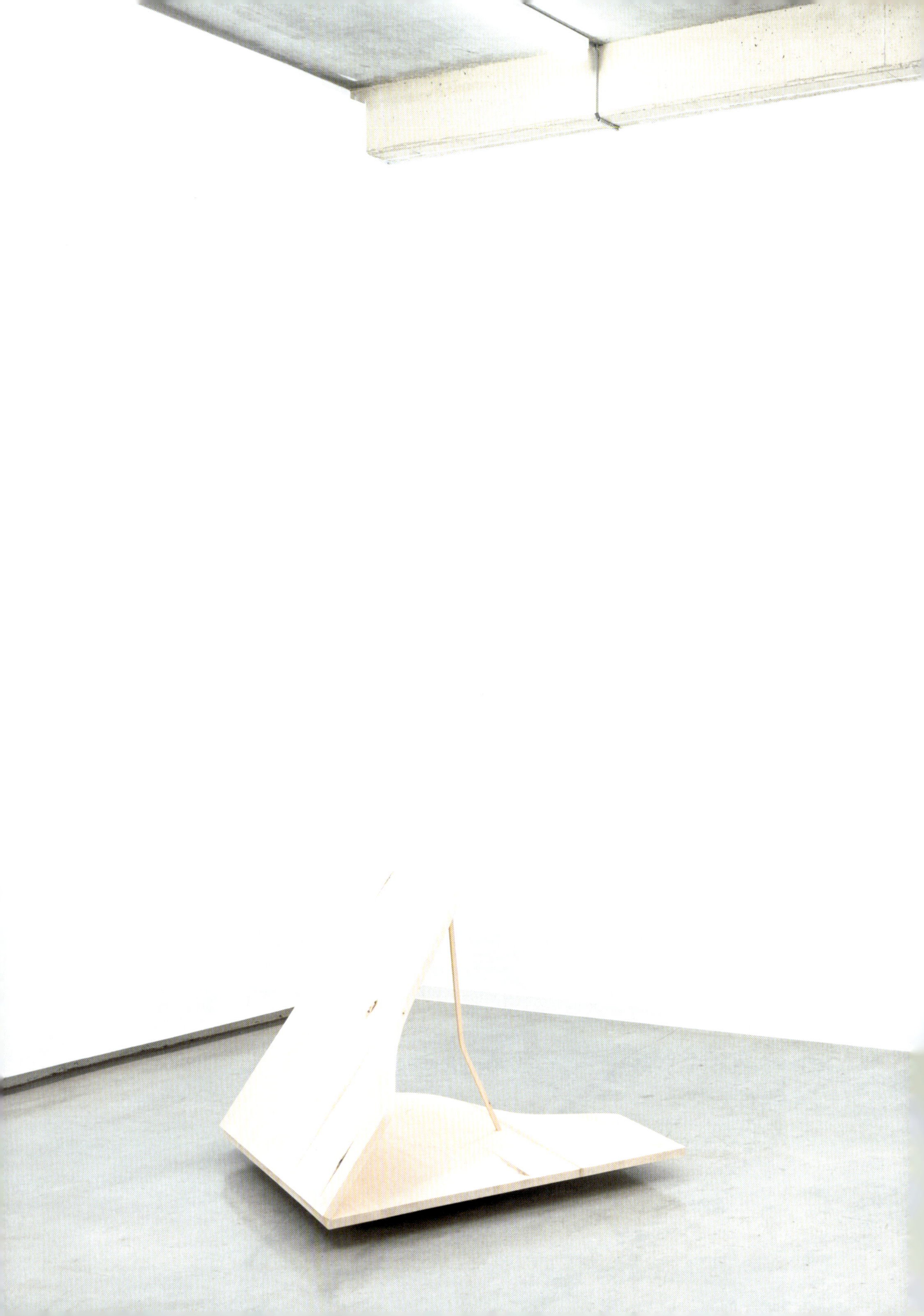

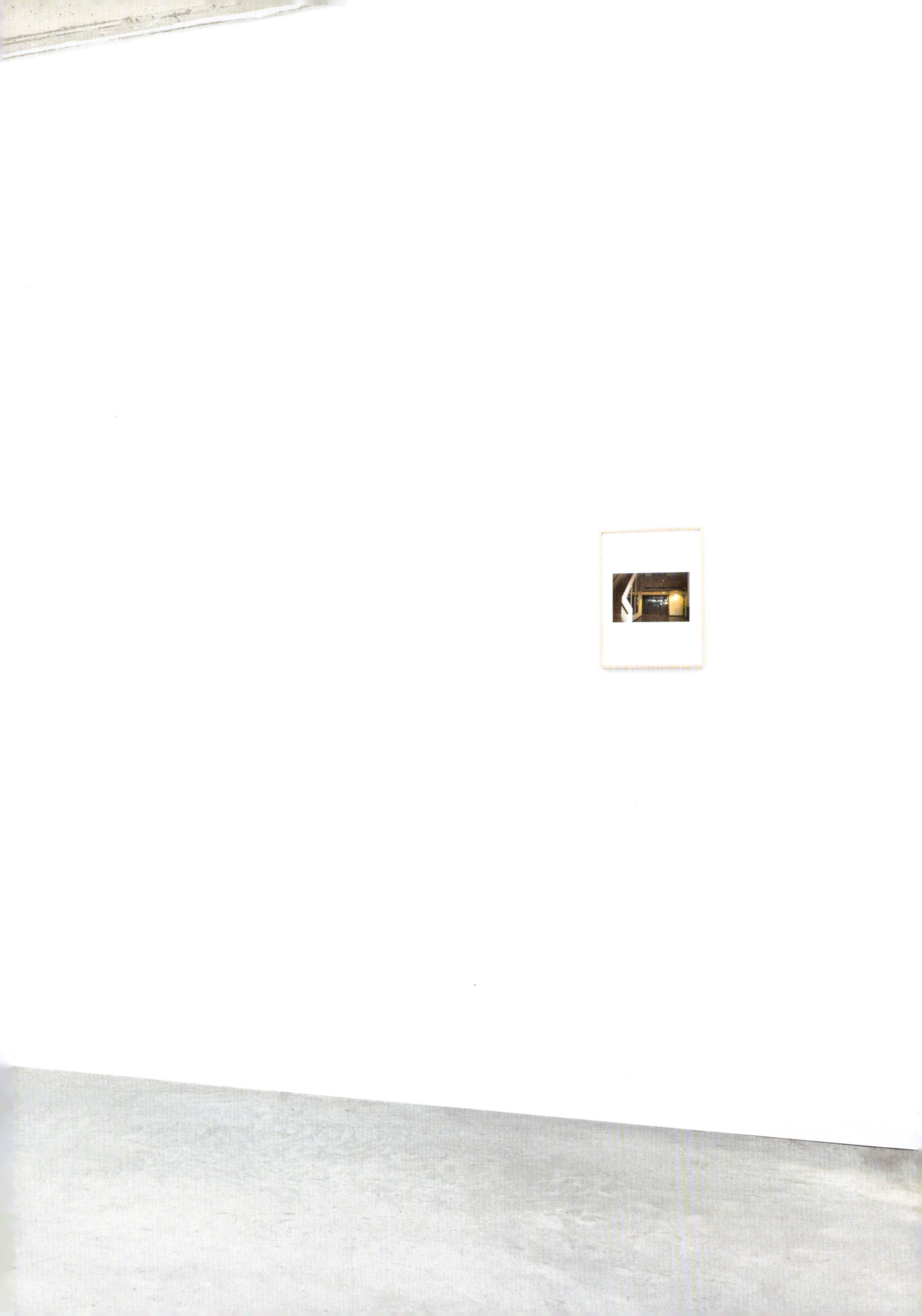

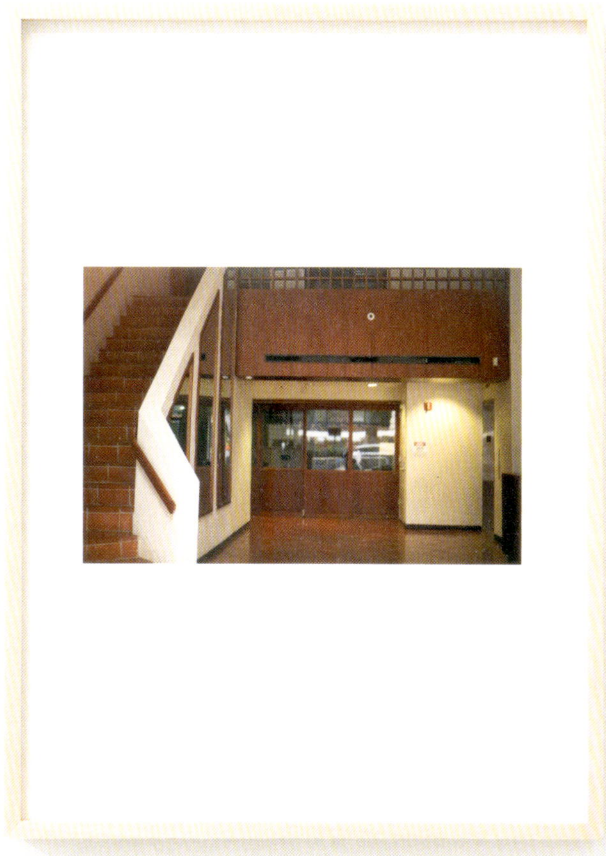

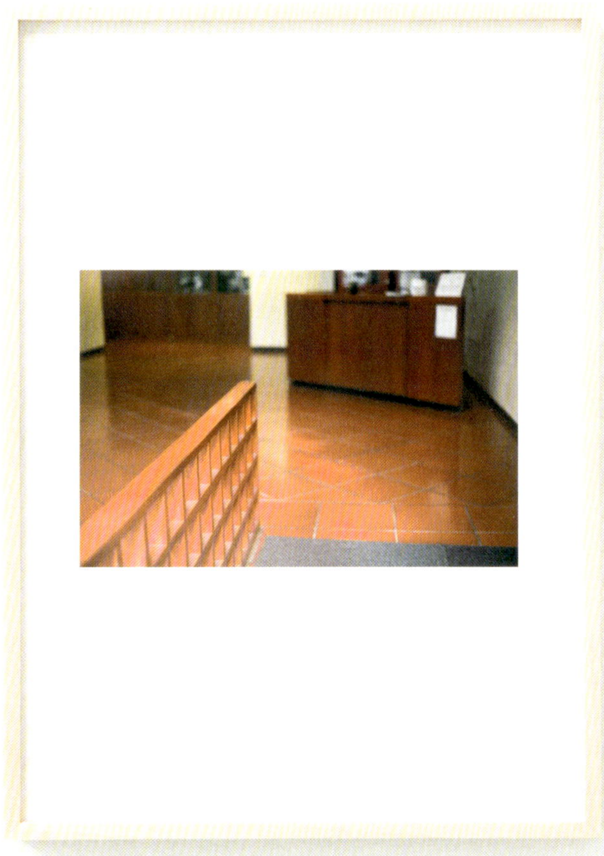

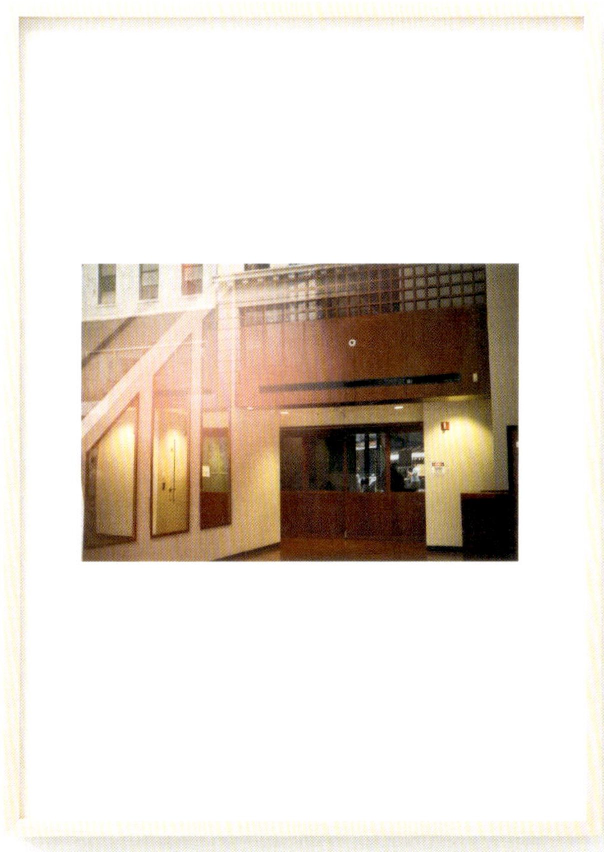

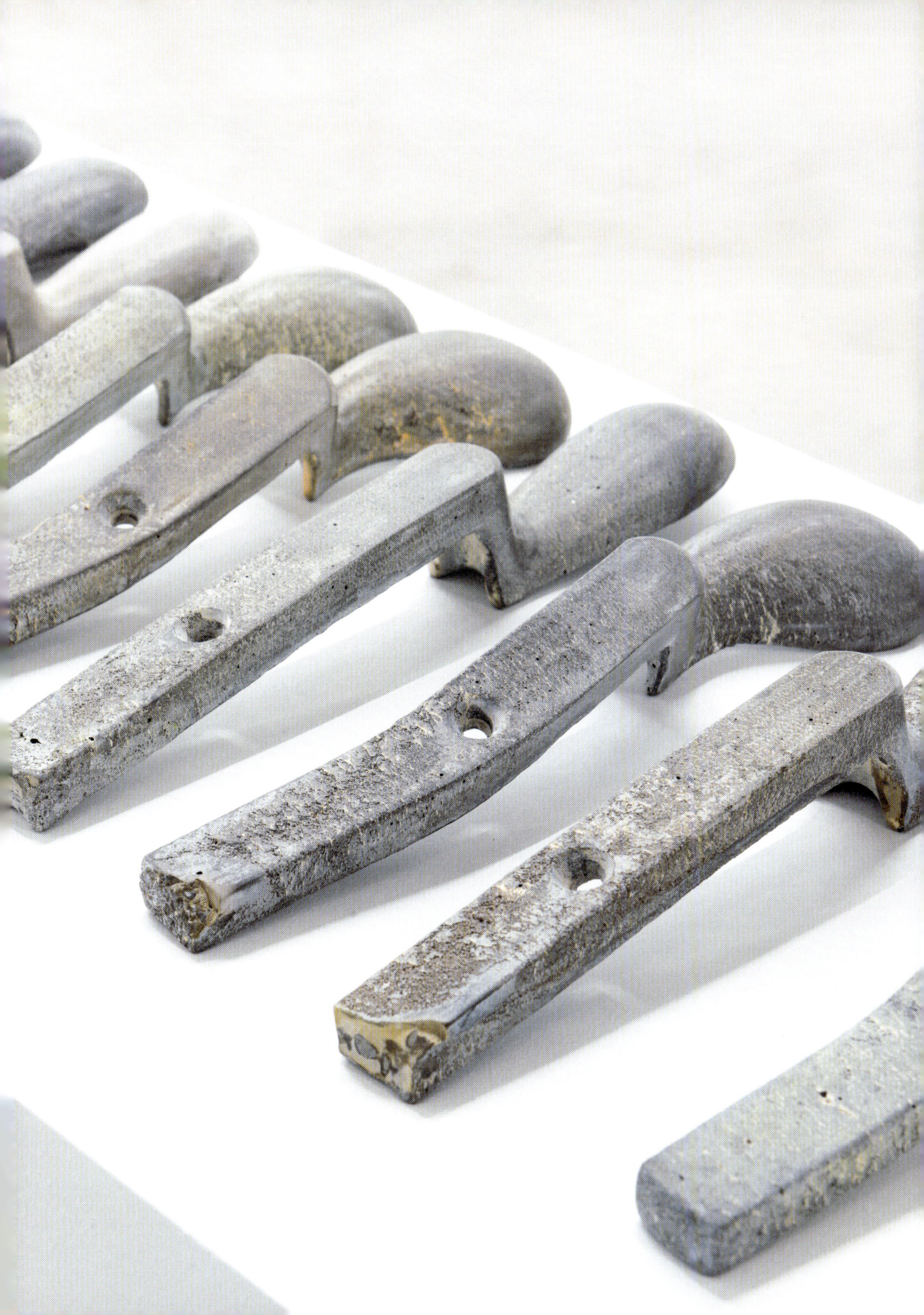

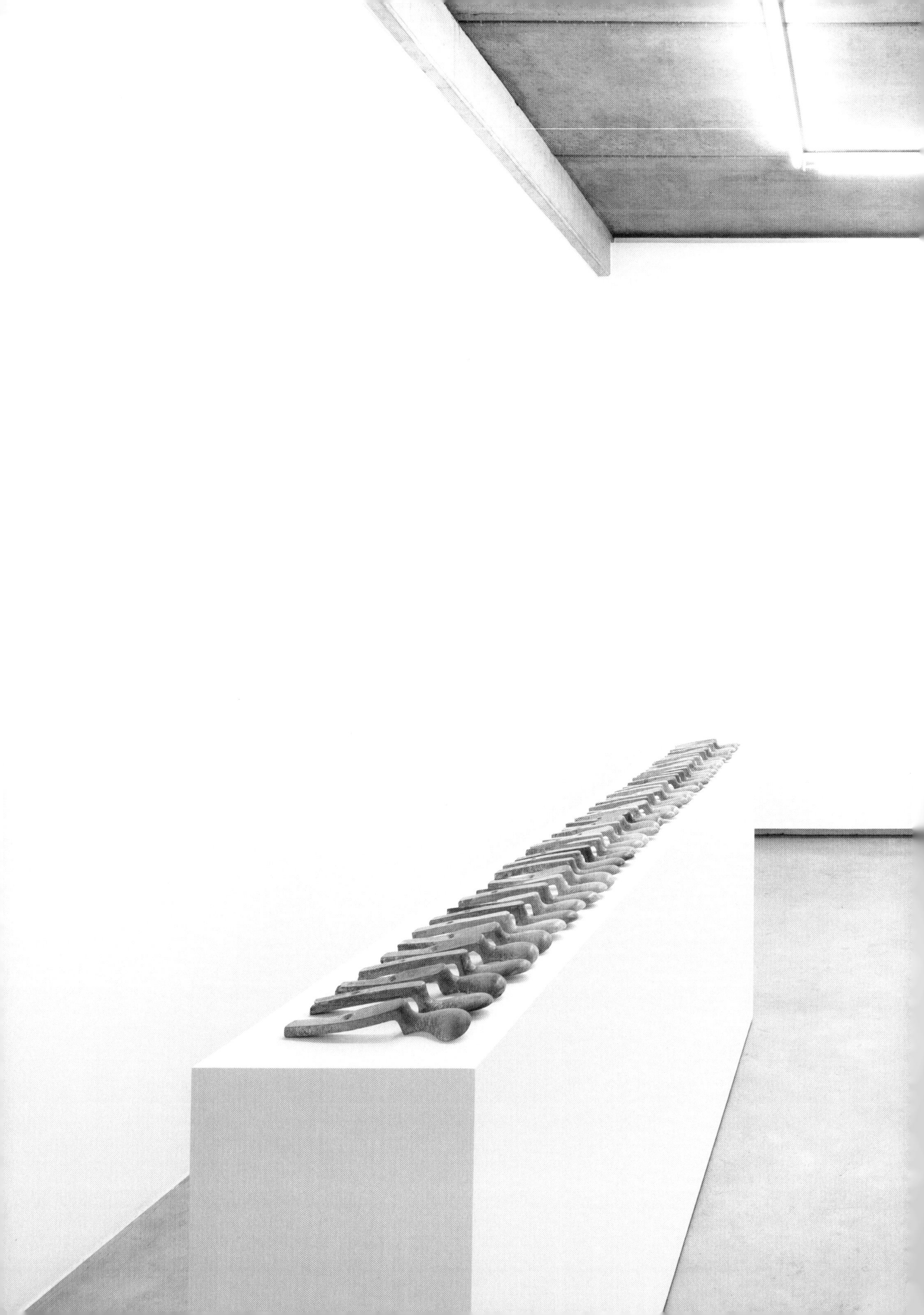

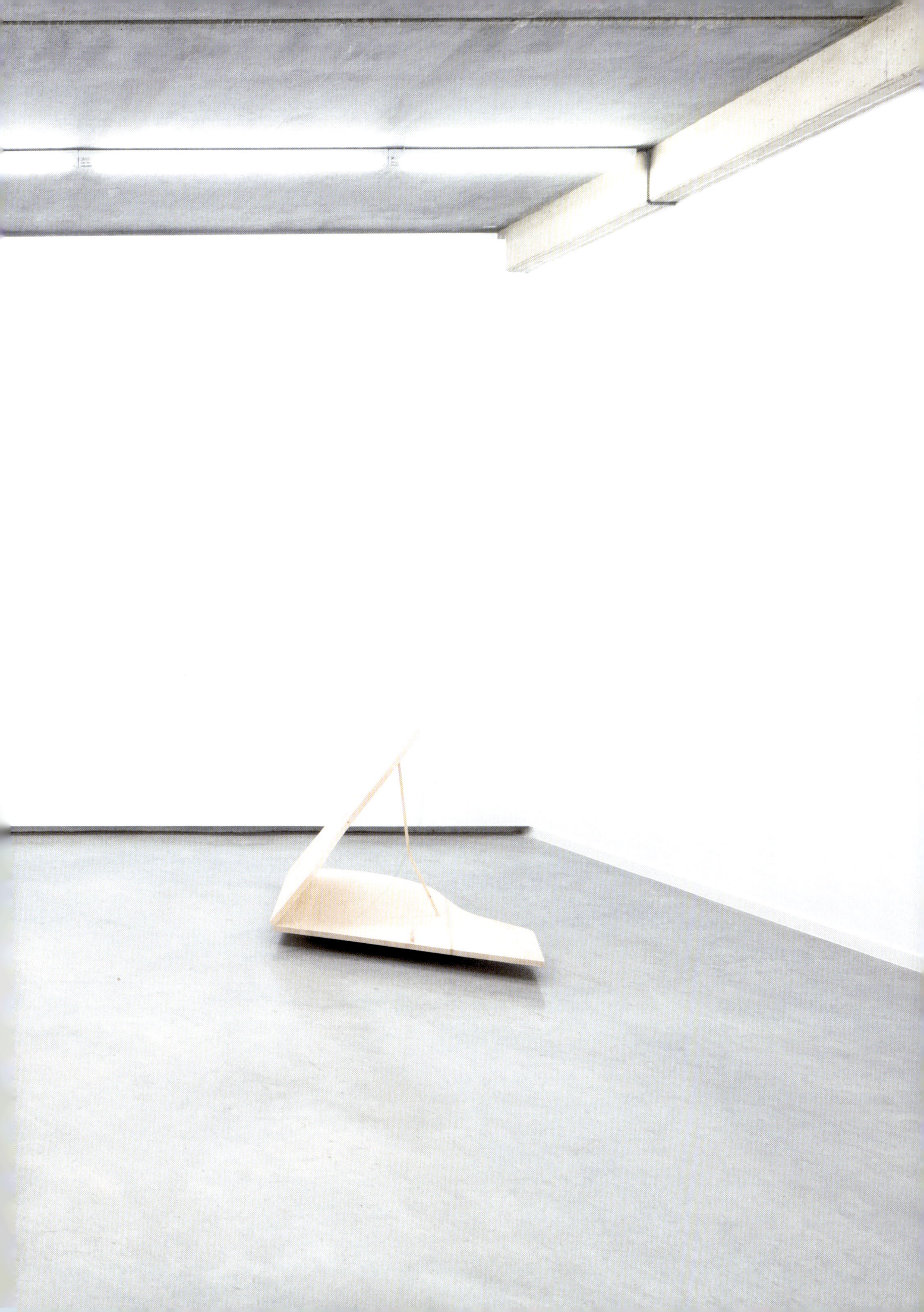

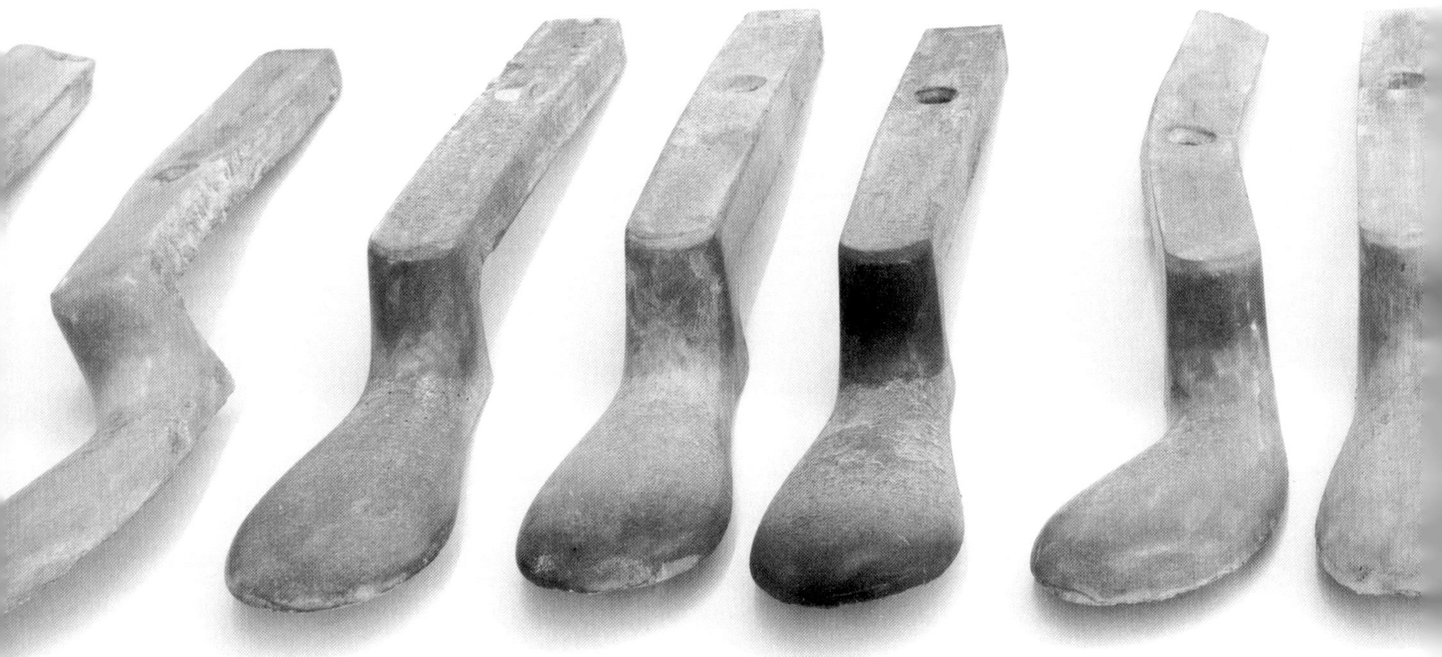

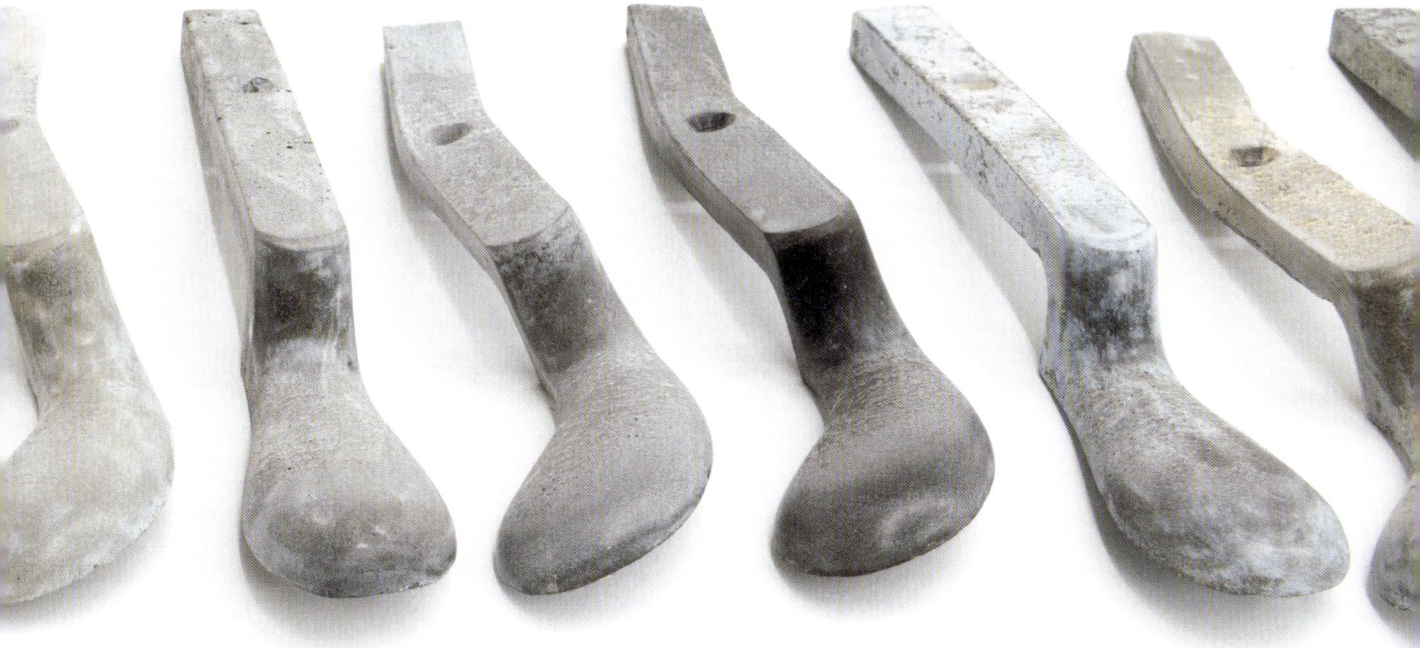

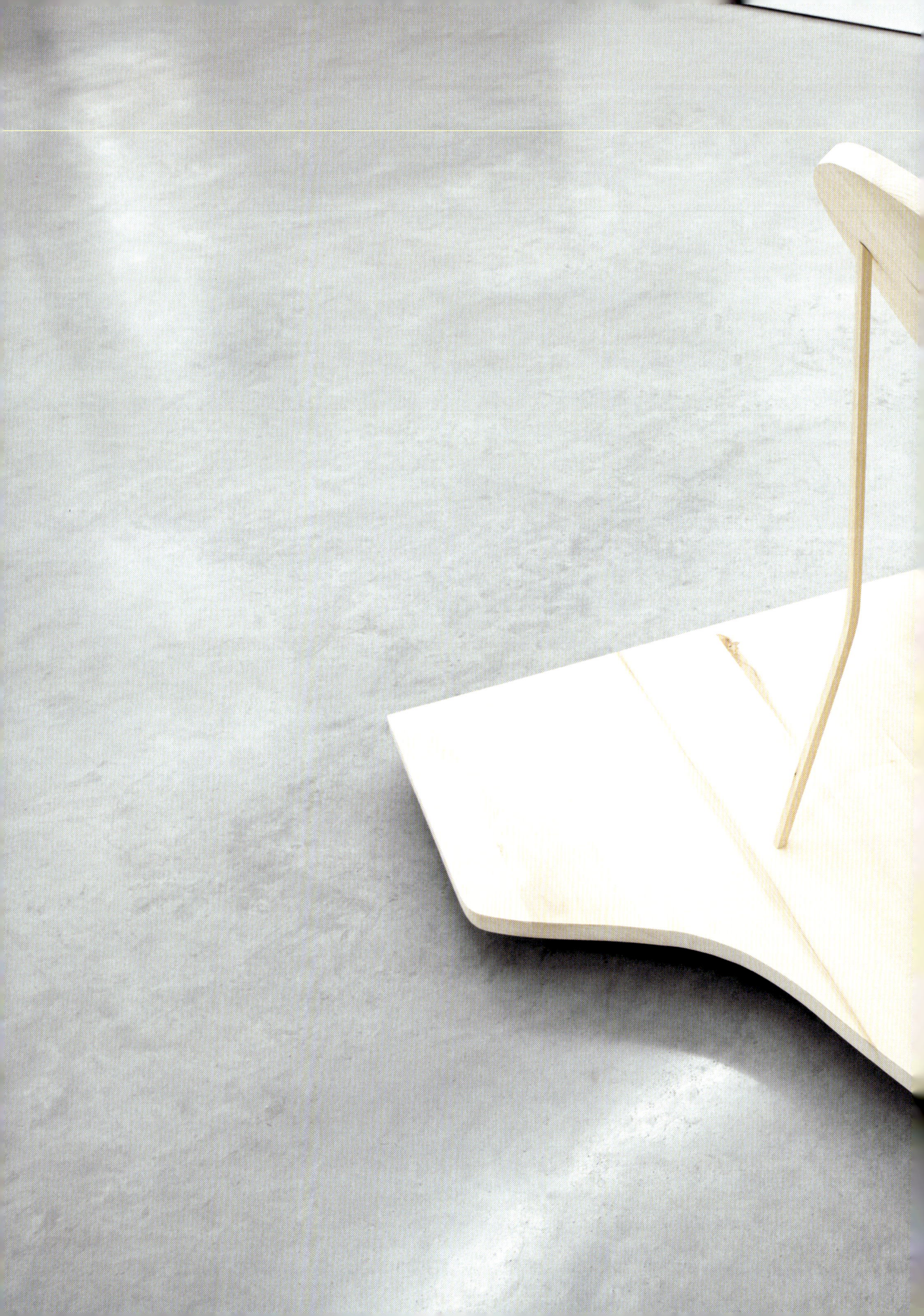

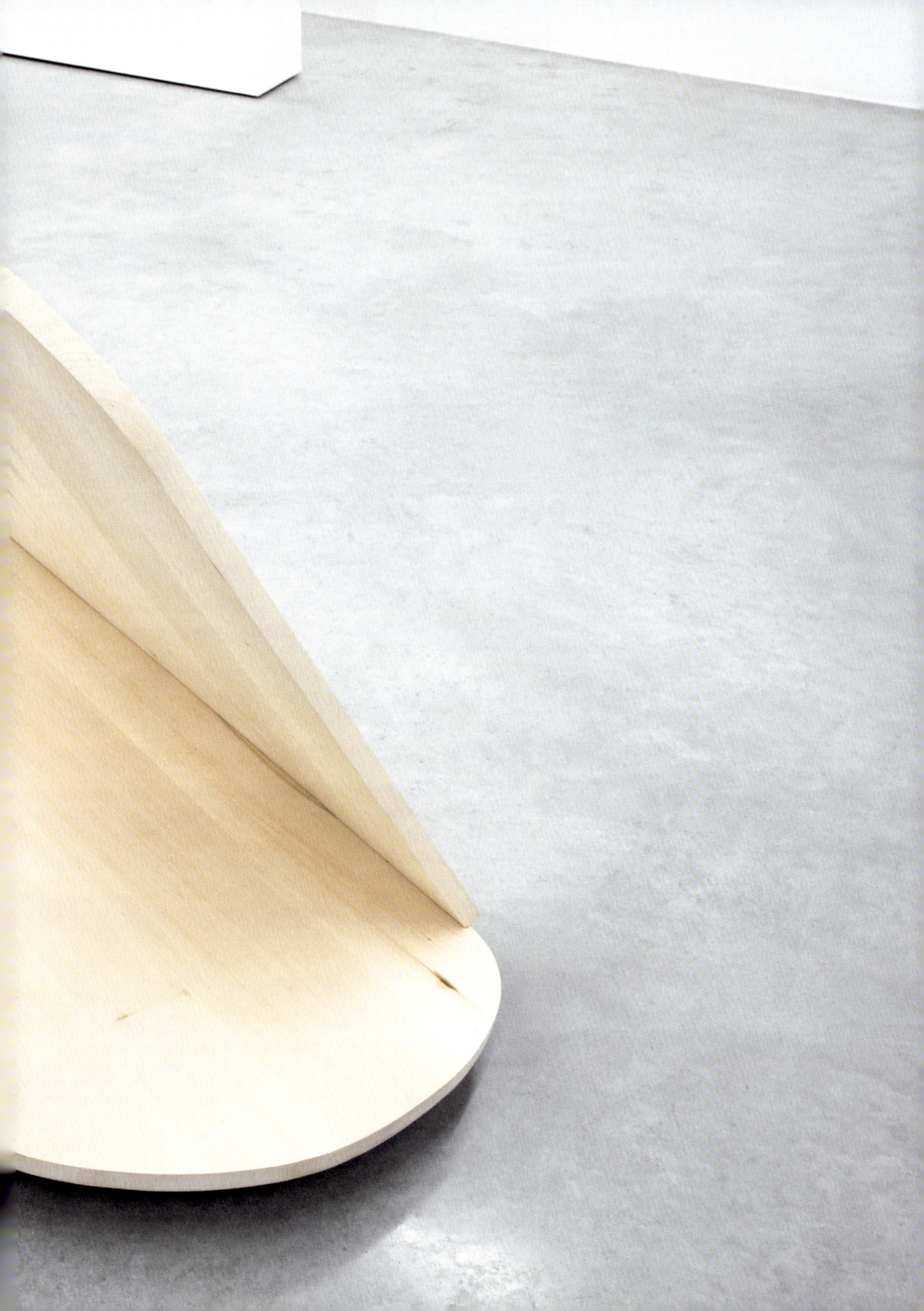

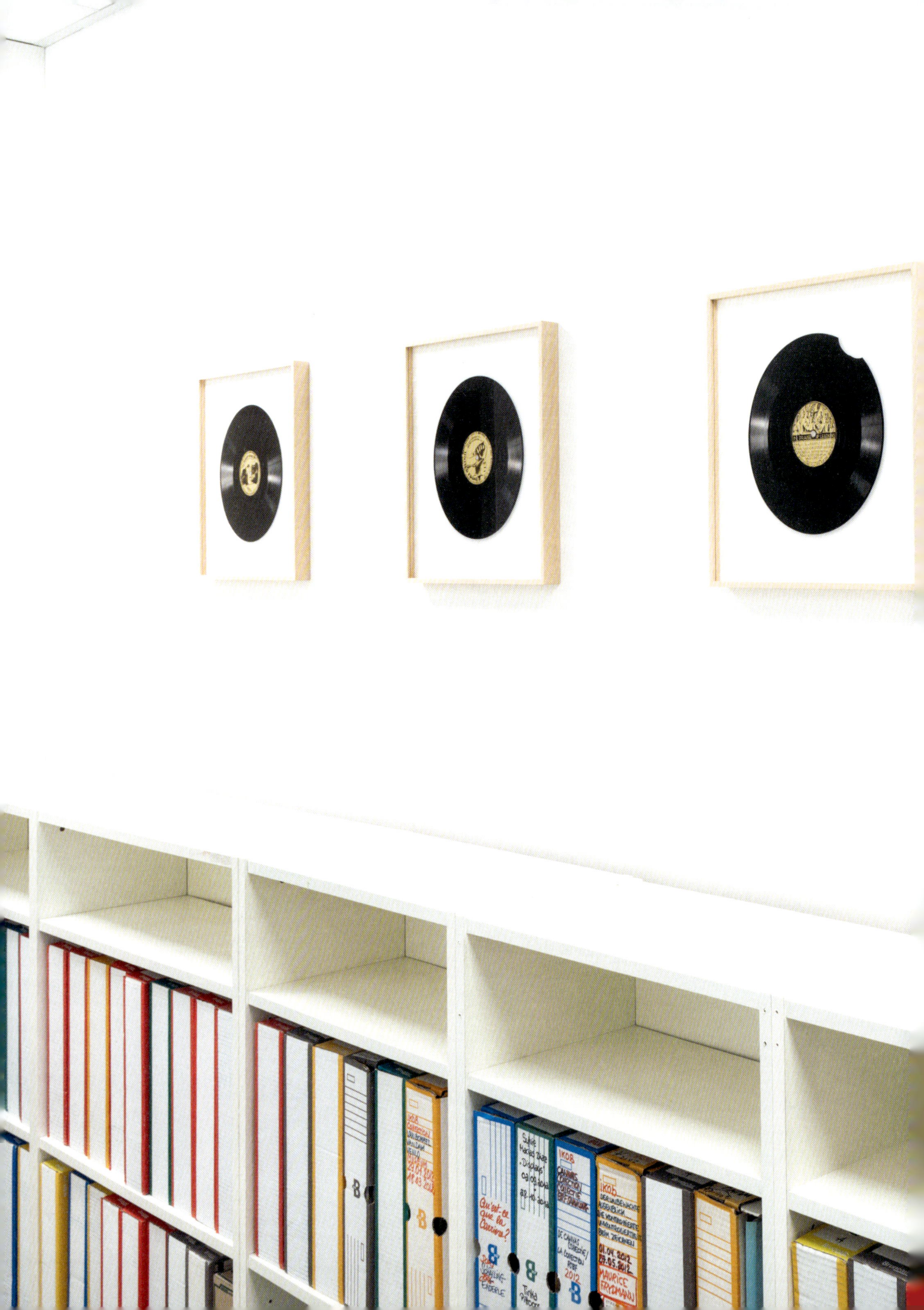

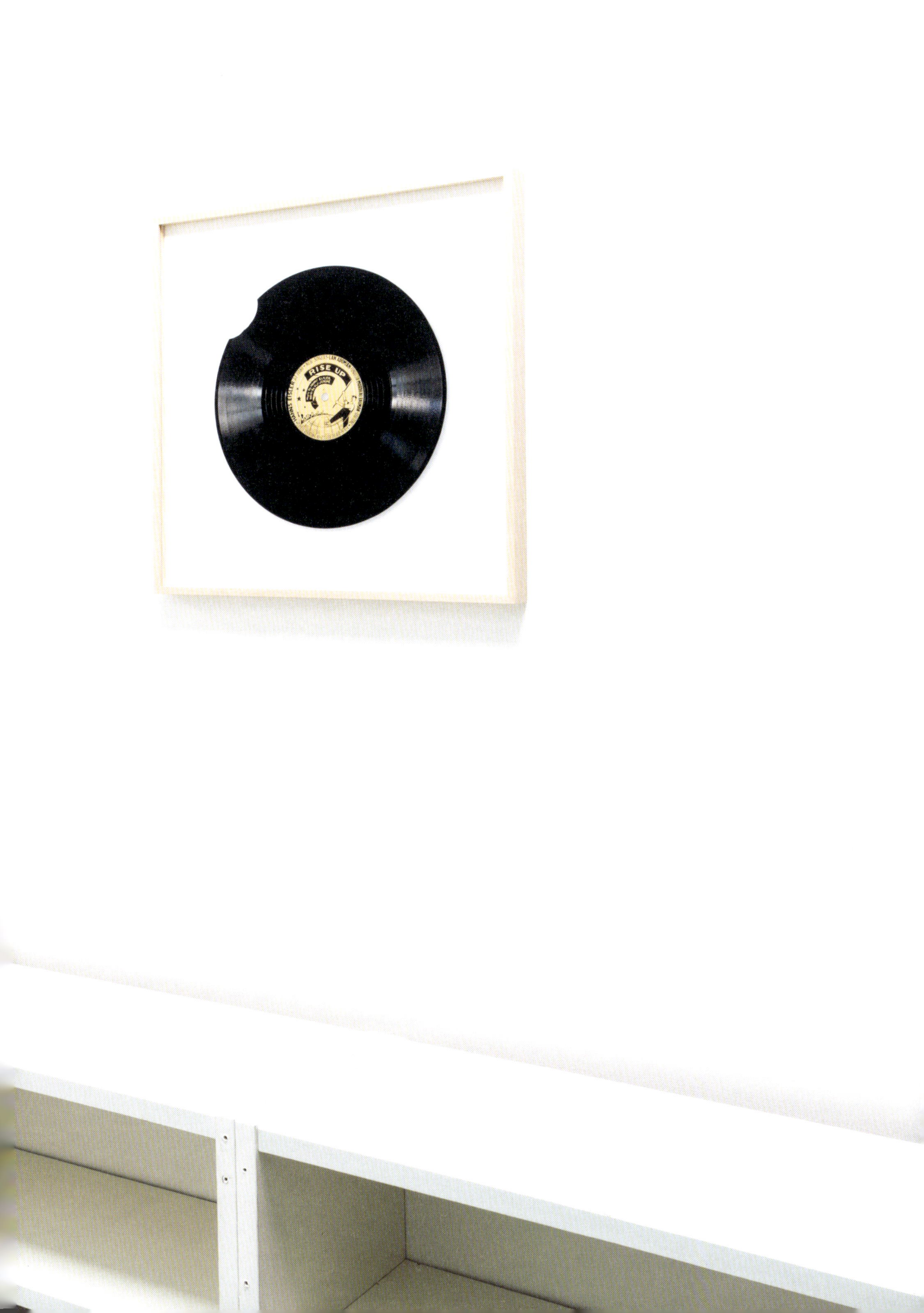
RISE UP

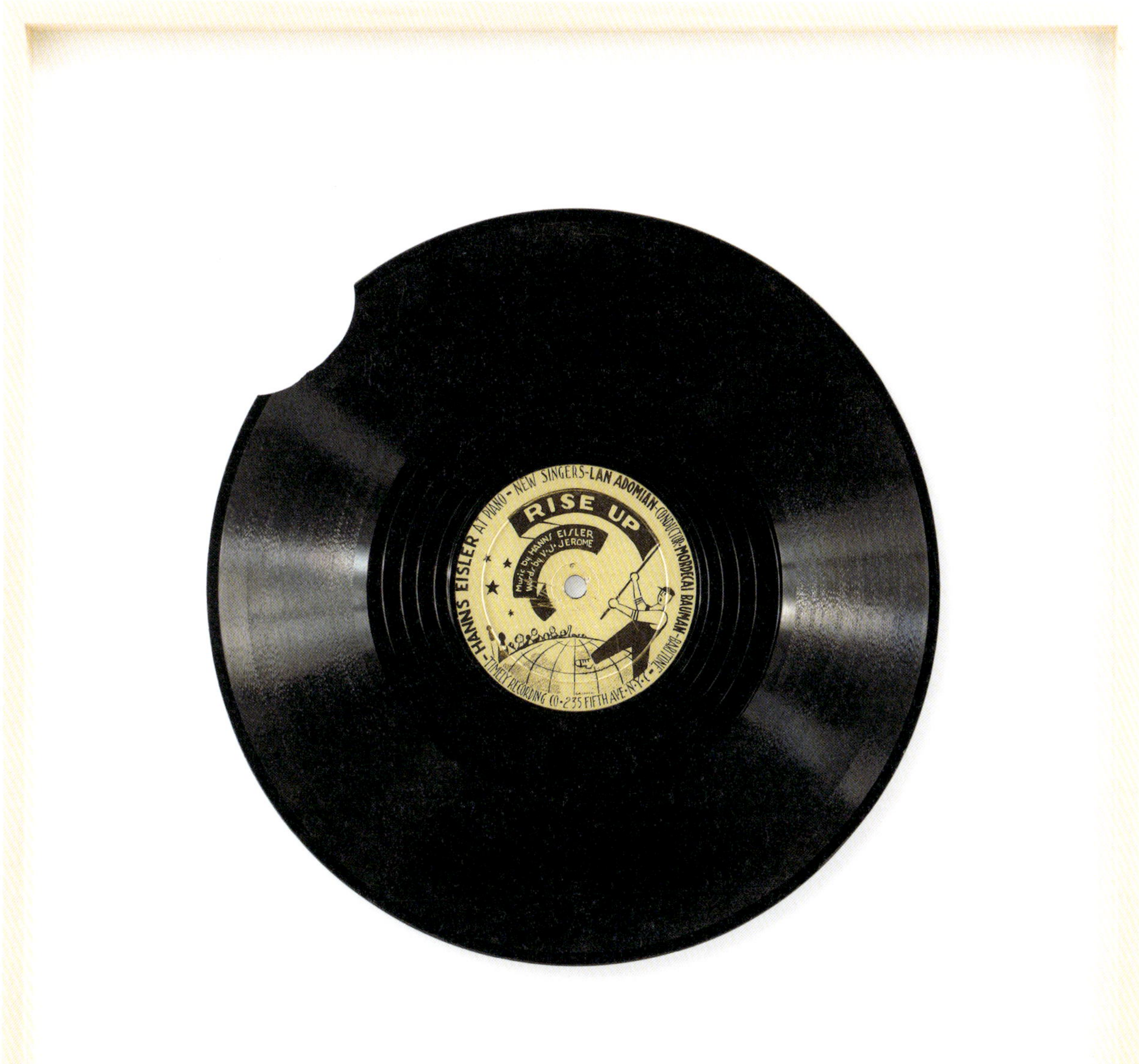
RISE UP
Music by HANNS EISLER
Words by V. J. JEROME
-HANNS EISLER AT PIANO - NEW SINGERS-LAN ADOMIAN-CONDUCTOR-MORDECAI BAUMAN-BARITONE-
-TIMELY RECORDING CO.-235 FIFTH AVE. N.Y.C.-

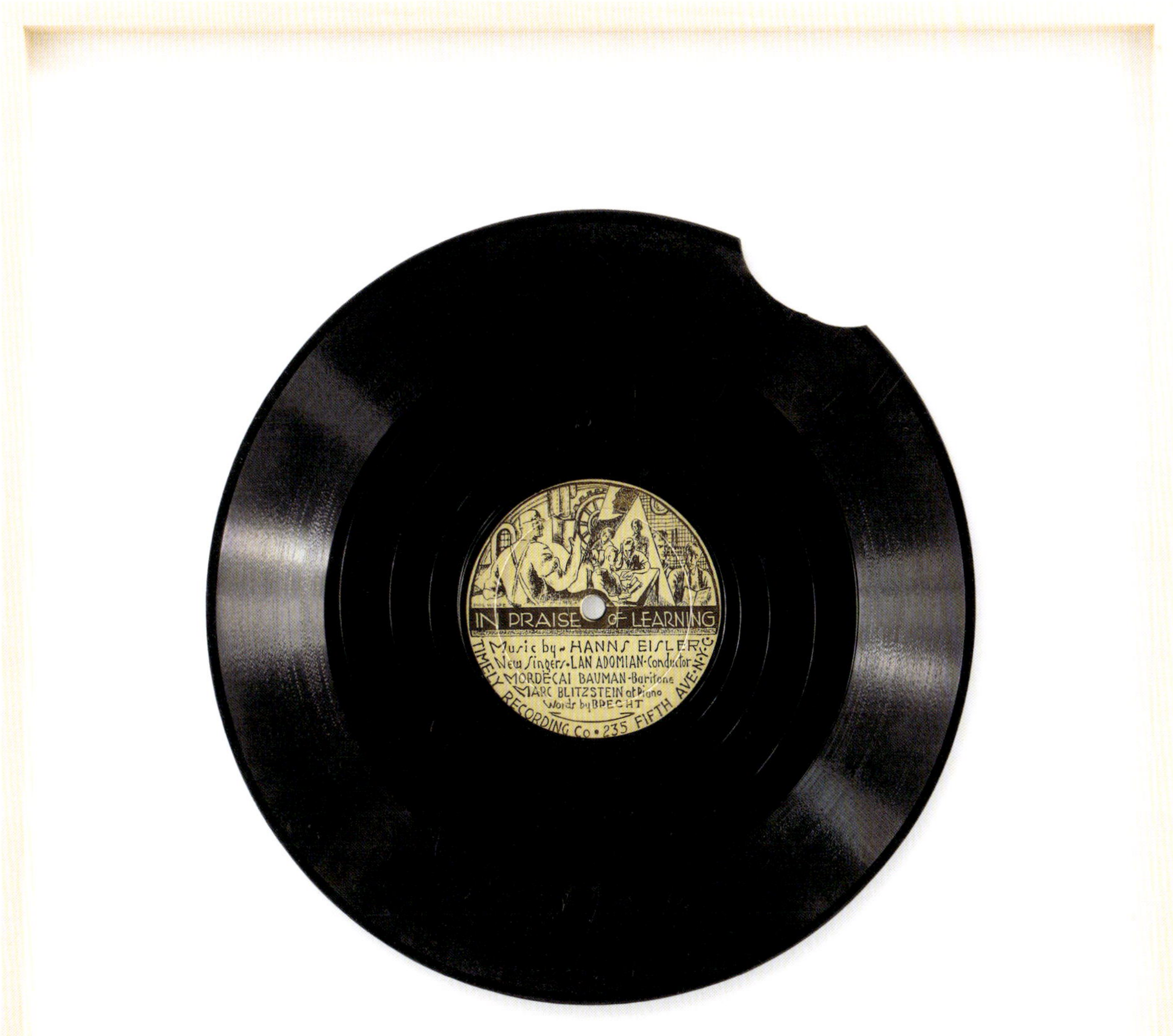
IN PRAISE OF LEARNING
Music by - HANNS EISLER
New Singers - LAN ADOMIAN - Conductor
MORDECAI BAUMAN - Baritone
MARC BLITZSTEIN at Piano
Words by BRECHT
TIMELY RECORDING Co • 235 FIFTH AVE • N.Y.C.

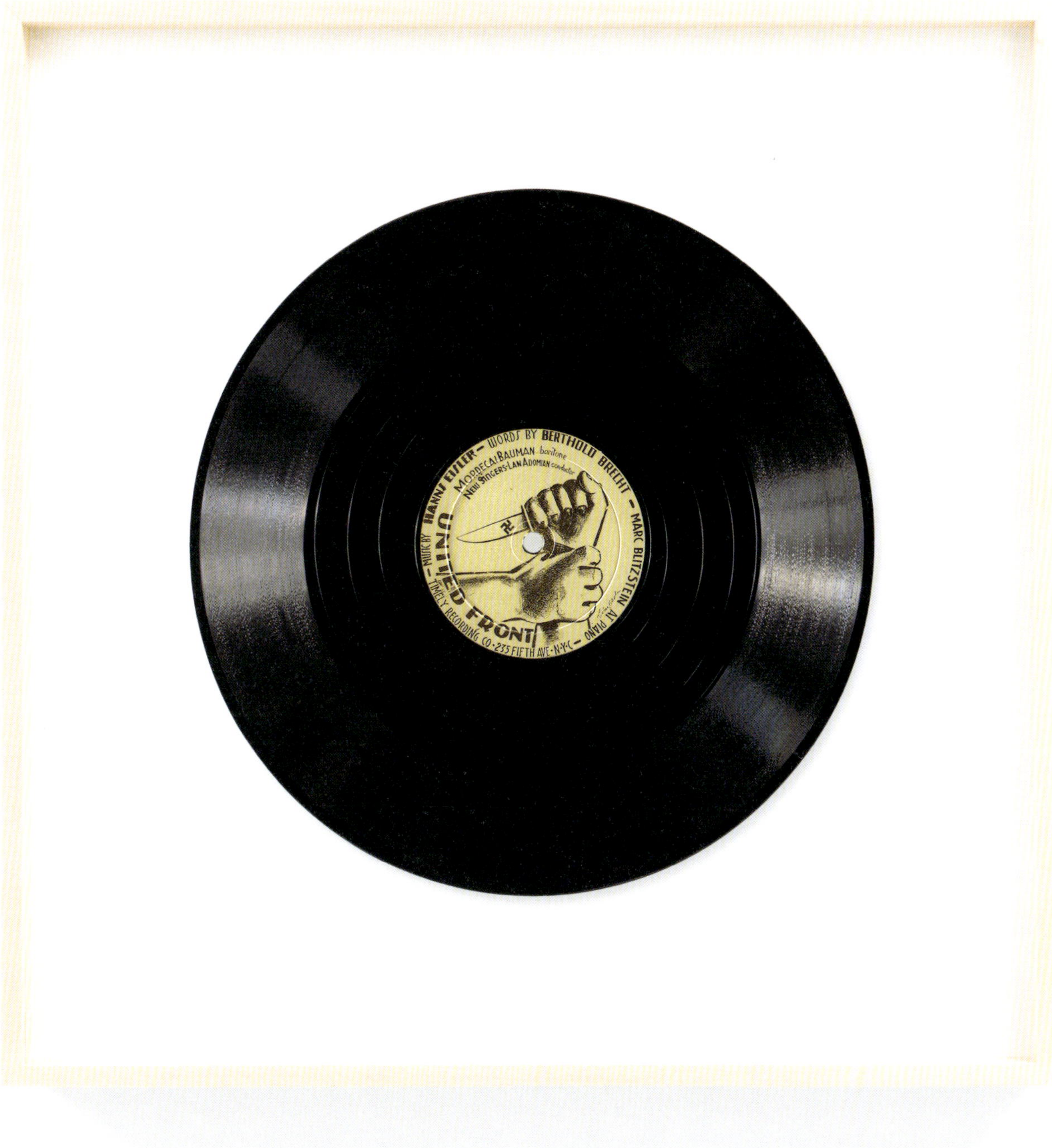
– MUSIC BY HANNS EISLER – WORDS BY BERTHOLD BRECHT – MARC BLITZSTEIN AT PIANO –
MORDECAI BAUMAN baritone
NEW SINGERS-LAN ADOMIAN conductor
UNITED FRONT
TIMELY RECORDING CO · 235 FIFTH AVE · N · Y · C

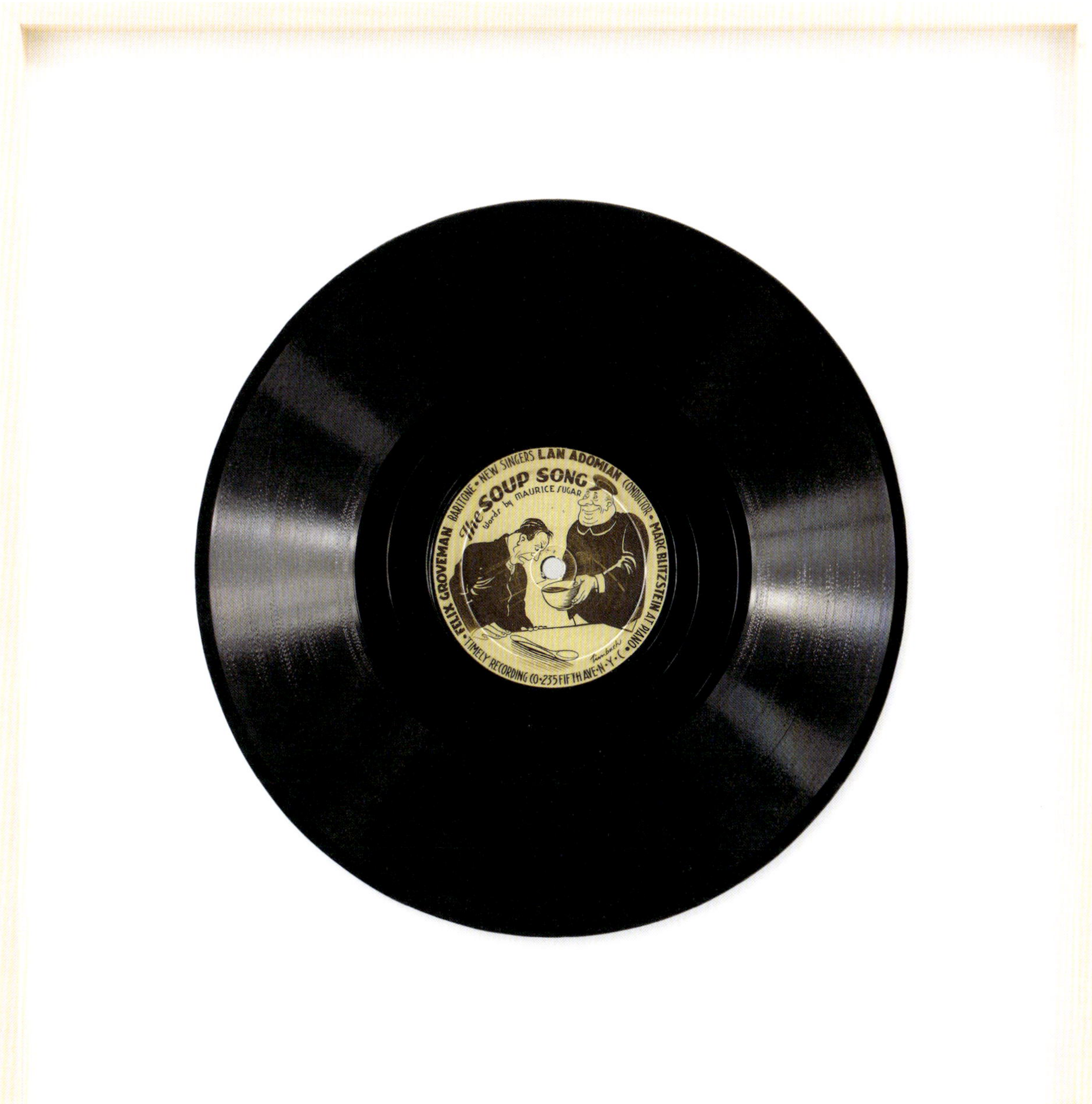
FELIX GROVEMAN BARITONE • NEW SINGERS LAN ADOMIAN CONDUCTOR • MARC BLITZSTEIN AT PIANO
The SOUP SONG
Words by MAURICE SUGAR
• TIMELY RECORDING CO • 235 FIFTH AVE • N • Y • C

The Blacklist

Ian F. Svenonius

A “blacklist” is an index of people or groups barred from employment by a particular industry, typically for some political affiliation or belief.

The list is “black,” i.e., invisible, top-secret, and officially dismissed as myth. The blacklist’s power to control and suppress stems largely, in fact, from its mysterious character and the rumors surrounding its existence or non-existence. Though the list is feared and its effects onerous, its veracity is unsubstantiated and it can always be plausibly denied by the ones doing the blacklisting.

Without evidence that one has been “blacklisted” – that one’s unemployment is due to ideological discrimination – the marginalized individual can be characterized as a bitter crank or paranoid. Perhaps their lack of success is actually a reflection of the poor quality of their work; or even of their character. Under Protestantism after all, wealth and success are clear indications of God’s favor, while poverty and failure exemplify the justice of a market which is intrinsically moral. Goodness is rewarded and venality is punished by the moral market (God) according to the ideology of capitalism/Protestantism. As a version of St Peter’s list at the gate of Heaven, the *blacklist* is popular with the ruling class. It furthers the bourgeoisie’s self-image as Gods who can choose who deserves to live or die.

The blacklist was utilized during the Industrial Revolution by mine and factory owners against union organizers and labor agitators, and led many to financial ruin, exile, and suicide. Though typically corporate, the military also uses blacklists to ensure that free-thinkers and non-conformists are dead-ended.

The Hollywood Blacklist, the best known of all the blacklists, destroyed a generation of "fellow traveller" intellectuals who were suspected of infecting audiences with insidious propaganda and communist ideology. It also destroyed the creative soul and spirit of the Hollywood film industry.

Indeed, with the House Un-American Activities Committee's (HUAC) 1947 investigation of the film industry, and subsequent banishment of suspected communists *(Joseph Losey, Hanns Eisler, Bertolt Brecht, Lillian Hellman, Jules Dassin, Dalton Trumbo, Ring Lardner, et al.)*, and its promotion of right-wing finks who ratted out colleagues and friends *(e.g. Elia Kazan, Budd Schulberg, Martin Berkeley, et al.)*, the movies that America proffered became more formulaic, moralistic, and dull minded. Hollywood endings, patriotic fables, and clumsy morality plays became the order of the day, as Cold War catatonia put an end to the glimmer of the Golden Age. The studios had historically sought out innovation and vision and had drafted the best and the brightest of Central and Eastern Europe's avant-garde for work in the "Dream Factory." Now, dreading exile and erasure, they opted to wallow in provincial fascism. Hollywood's aesthetic collapse led to the rise of Euro art-house cinema as discontented movie-goers increasingly sought out sexier, more philosophical, and generally less idiotic fare in French, Swedish, and Italian cinema.

Though the blacklist is popularly said to have ended in 1960 with Dalton Trumbo's public accreditation as screenplay writer of *Spartacus* (based on a novel written by blacklisted author Howard Fast) it, in fact, didn't end but just became mundane; an accepted reality of life. The HUAC affair had a chilling effect on artistic and political expression in the USA. Afterwards, the population understood that the much touted "free speech" and "freedom of political expression" were privileges that one should enjoy very selectively, if at all. One could be an anti-authoritarian rebel of course, just as long as it was in the right way. The "arts" were, Post-War, entirely infiltrated and co-opted by the newly established CIA (created the same year as the HUAC hearings) who would later boast, loudly and often, of having invented Abstract Expressionism, publishing *The Paris Review*, and so on.

While these front operations are retold as quaint tales from Cold War antiquity, the CIA's infiltration of academia and the arts has ironically increased since the end of the Soviet Union. Recognizing these bourgeois institutions as being central to indoctrination of the culture at large, Langley works diligently to construct and celebrate aesthetic narratives that rehabilitate Washington's imperial ideology. This hidden hand behind critical and cultural trends has wiped away the conceits of modernism and reinvented the art world as an exclusive dinner party where very particular conversations can be had. Propaganda politics are all the rage as long as they preclude critique of the war machine and the oligarchy and instead focus their contempt on the working class.

Though the CIA still works behind the scenes, as a kind of covert Medici family, its opponents are always changing in a topsy turvy world of ever changing alliances/enemies. The art that is commissioned for the new ideological battleground, of course, changes accordingly. Blacklists are in use still but – in the absence of a communist threat – are utilized against disposable celebrity sacrifices, randomly selected according to vague sins of comportment. Aesthetic critique has transferred from the artworks on the wall to the artist's character or personality as it pertains to ever changing fads and styles.

The blacklist model – popularly recognized as fact but officially denied – led to a de facto self-censorship in the arts and in life. Nonconformity obediently took on prescribed forms; jazz beatnik, rock'n'roll rebel, narcotic user, religious eccentric, sexual deviant, and whiskey head were insubordinations which were celebrated and institutionalized by the culture industry, but political disobedience was to be shunned, condemned, and despised. The propaganda of the post-war era was virulent in its institutionalization of rebellion as a purely apolitical and emotionalist pastime (*The Wild One,* László Benedek, 1953, *Rebel Without a Cause,* Nicholas Ray, 1955, *On the Road,* Jack Kerouac, 1957, et al.).

The arts have all been colonized by the State. In the wake of the blacklist and the HUAC hearings, Hollywood has found its greatest financier in the Pentagon and the Pentagon's main competitor, the CIA/State Department. These institutions are now Hollywood's most reliable financiers, counted on for production of the fascistic ultra violent interventionist white savior imperialist brainwashing blockbusters that are the cineplex's mainstays.

The Hollywood blacklist was the first volley in the Cold War, which began in earnest in 1948, the year of the P.L.A. (People's Liberation Army) victory in China and the E.L.A.S. (Greek People's Liberation Army) defeat in Greece. These two struggles cemented the divisions between "East" and "West" i.e. the struggle between bourgeois imperialism and the decolonization movements which were being financed and encouraged by the USSR.

The Cold War expressed itself in proxy wars, espionage, revolutions, art and film. Both the East and the West put enormous resources into shaping a cultural export which would sway undecided inhabitants of the contested planet toward their particular ideology. While the Bolsheviks bet on the strategy of high art for the masses, focusing on ballet, theater, poetry and symphonic music, the Americans went for an institutionalization of low-brow culture (i.e., jazz, rock'n'roll, comics, etc.) to win over the global proletariat and the intelligentsia. Susan Sontag's "Notes on Camp" (1964) was a manifesto for this institutionalized refutation of high art, which was in fact a celebration of the market as an intrinsically enlightened, cleansing force; the conceit of Protestantism/capitalism. "Pop Art," though mistaken as a critique of commercialism, was in fact a paean to it. Though the communist project was destroyed by 1991, with the fall of the USSR and the absorption of the PRC into a neoliberal framework, "the blacklist" is still extant so as to guard against possible future dissent.

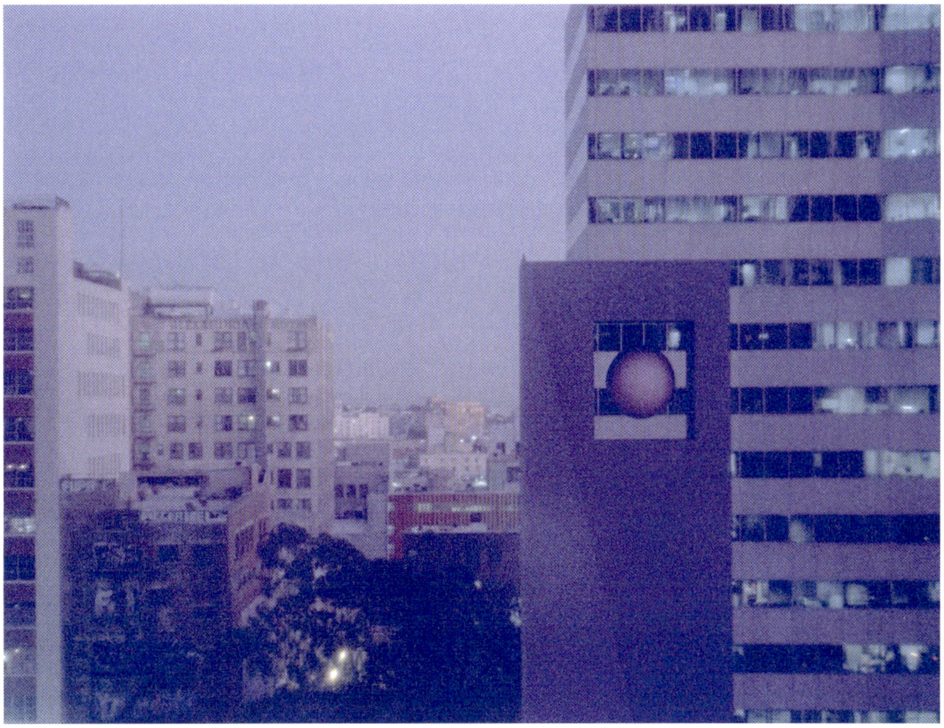

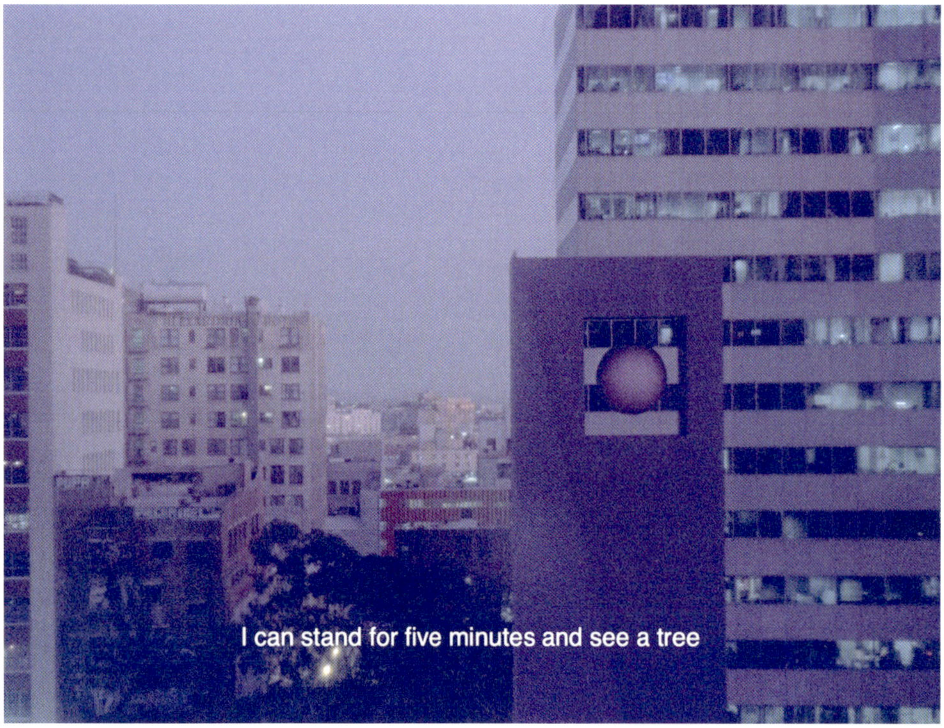
I can stand for five minutes and see a tree

Die ganze Wüste ist eine Pause

Brenda Guesnet

1 Quinn Latimer, „Kalifornien träumen: Bertolt Brecht's LA Poetry, and Other Sunstruck Germanic Specters", in: *Like a Woman: Essays, Readings, Poems* [Übersetzung aus dem Englischen]. Berlin / London: Sternberg Press, 2017, S. 27.

2 So waren zum Beispiel das „Solidaritätslied" (1931) und das „Einheitsfrontlied" (1934), beide mit Texten von Brecht, einprägsame Hymnen zum Mitsingen für die Arbeiterbewegung.

3 Mike Davis, *City of Quartz: Excavating the Future in Los Angeles*, London, New York: Verso Books, 1990.

4 Theodor Adorno, Hanns Eisler, *Composing for the Films*, New York: Oxford University Press, 1947.

5 Christa Blümlinger, „The Filmed Body and the Cinematic Gesture: Zoe Beloff's Revisions", in: *European Journal of Media Studies*, NECSUS 8 (2), Autumn 2019: 169–188 URL: https://necsus-ejms.org/

6 Jennifer Egan, „Great Rock and Roll Pauses by Alison Blake", in: *A Visit from the Goon Squad*, New York: Knopf, 2010.

7 Es gibt zwei Versionen des Films *Garten sprengen*, eine für das Kino mit Abspann und eine zweite für den Ausstellungskontext, die kontinuierlich im Loop läuft und daher keine Credits enthält.

„Garten sprengen“
ist eine mehrdeutige Wendung,

offen für nuancierte Lesarten: Ich höre sie als einen *explodierenden Garten*, aber auch seine *Bewässerung* kann so zum Ausdruck gebracht werden. Der Titel von Veronika Eberharts Film und ihrer gleichnamigen Ausstellung im IKOB – Museum für Zeitgenössische Kunst in Belgien bezieht sich auf Bertolt Brechts Gedicht „Vom Sprengen des Gartens“ aus dem Jahr 1942, das der Komponist Hanns Eisler später vertonen würde:

> *O Sprengen des Gartens, das Grün zu ermutigen!*
> *Wässern der durstigen Bäume! Gib mehr als genug.*

Als Brecht diese Zeilen verfasste, lebte er im Exil in Los Angeles, das Gedicht ist Teil seiner „Hollywoodelegien“. Die offensichtlichen Widersprüche der Stadt saugte er auf und ließ sie in zahlreiche Metaphern einfließen. Das viele Grün in seiner Umgebung beschäftigte ihn: Er war zugleich fasziniert und beunruhigt angesichts der vielen Parks und Gärten, die Unmengen von Wasser und teure Bewässerungssysteme benötigten, um inmitten der Wüste am Leben zu bleiben. Wie die Pflanzen war Brecht selbst, ebenso wie die vielen anderen Deutschsprachigen im Exil (darunter Hanns Eisler, Peter Lorre, Fritz Lang, Theodor W. Adorno, Salka Viertel, Arnold Schönberg und Heinrich Mann), ein unwahrscheinlicher Bewohner von Los Angeles. Sie waren Vertreter der europäischen Avantgarde, die, in den Worten der amerikanischen Schriftstellerin Quinn Latimer, „von den Schlachtfeldern im Europa des Zweiten Weltkrieges flohen und sich in einer Stadt von Engeln am azurblauen Becken des Pazifiks wiederfanden.“[1]

Brechts wichtigster künstlerische Partner zu dieser Zeit war der deutsch-österreichische Komponist Hanns Eisler (1898–1962). Die beiden hatten sich 1930 kennengelernt, fortan komponierte Eisler die Musik für viele von Brechts Texten bzw. Stücken. Als überzeugter Marxist sah Eisler in der Musik ein wirksames Instrument, um die sozialistische Weltanschauung zu artikulieren und massenwirksam zu transportieren. Text und Ton sollten komplementär eingesetzt werden und wirkungsvoll politische Botschaften vermitteln. Eisler fügte Elemente populärer und klassischer Musik zusammen und komponierte so politisch engagierte Musik, die der Mobilisierung der Arbeiterklasse für die Revolution dienen sollte.[2]

Da sich die Lebensbedingungen für Jüd·innen, aber auch für linke Künstler·innen sowohl in Deutschland als auch in Österreich zunehmend verschlechterten, emigrierte Eisler 1938 in die Vereinigten Staaten. Brecht folgte im Jahr 1941. In Los Angeles setzten die beiden ihre fruchtbare Zusammenarbeit fort, allen voran 1943 im Film *Hangmen Also Die!* unter der Regie von Fritz Lang. Eisler wurde für einen Academy Award in der Kategorie „Beste Filmmusik“ nominiert. Der Erfolg dieser drei deutschsprachigen Exilanten zeugt vom europäischen Einfluss auf die amerikanische Kultur. Es dauerte jedoch nicht lange, bis Eislers politische Ansichten anfingen, ihm in seiner neuen Heimat Probleme zu bereiten. Er und viele andere europäische Intellektuelle standen unter ständiger

Beobachtung des FBI, die sich in den folgenden Jahren noch verschärfte. 1947 wurde Eisler vom Komitee für unamerikanische Umtriebe (engl. HUAC: House Un-American Activities Committee) vorgeladen, verhört und beschuldigt, ein sowjetischer Agent zu sein. Ein Jahr später musste er das Land verlassen, kehrte zunächst nach Wien zurück und ließ sich letztendlich in der DDR nieder. Dort komponierte er 1949 das Lied „Auferstanden aus Ruinen“, das zur Nationalhymne der jungen Republik wurde.

Veronika Eberharts Film *Garten sprengen* aus dem Jahr 2022 spielt an dem Ort, an dem Eislers erste, geheime HUAC-Anhörungen stattgefunden haben: im Biltmore Hotel in Los Angeles. Elf Stockwerke hoch und einen halben Häuserblock einnehmend, dienten seine Ballsäle als Kulisse von Hollywood-Filmen und Oscar-Verleihungen. Eberhart richtet ihre 16mm Kamera auf die symbolischen Besonderheiten des Biltmores, die geschwungenen Treppen, die kunstvoll gemusterten Teppiche, die weitläufigen Speisesäle. So verbindet sie Themen rund um Eislers Biografie mit dem Reich der Traumfabrik. Los Angeles, die Spitze von urbaner Dialektik, von Sonnenschein und Noir, wie Mike Davis sagen würde,[3] wird mit Vorstellungen von Exil und drohender Zensur verwoben. Der nach innen gekehrte Blick bei gleichzeitig nach außen gerichteter, ausufernder Spurensuche ist charakteristisch für Eberharts Arbeitsweise. Spezifische historische Bezüge gepaart mit gründlicher Recherche und poetischen Impressionen fügt sie zu komplexen Arrangements künstlerischen Ausdrucks in Form von Videos, Skulpturen und Installationen zusammen. Von Goethes *Faust* und lacanianischen Offenbarungen im Baltimore bis zu ihrer Faszination für Eisler verwertet sie ihre Quellen geschickt und macht daraus wirkungsvolle Meditationen über Kunstgeschichte, Politik und Gesellschaft.

Garten sprengen erkundet das noch immer betriebene Biltmore Hotel als einen Ort kultureller Produktion: sowohl seine hochgradig prominente, im Fernsehen zu bewundernde Bühnenpräsenz als auch seine Funktion als Schauplatz streng geheimer Anhörungen, abgeschirmt und vor der Öffentlichkeit verborgen. In den Film eingearbeitet sind die Hotelszenen aus *Beverly Hills Cop* (1984) und *I Wanna Hold Your Hand* (1978) sowie Aufnahmen von Brechts und Eislers HUAC-Anhörungen (1947). Diese Episoden versteht man durch Eberharts Montage als integrale Bestandteile der Verwaltung dessen, was an kulturellem Ausdruck zulässig ist und was nicht. In der ersten Einstellung legt jemand eine Schallplatte auf, aber alles, was man zu hören bekommt, ist ein Rauschen. Damit rückt umgehend ein zentraler Punkt dieses bemerkenswerten 12-minütigen Films in den Vordergrund: die Bedeutsamkeit von Stille, Pausen und Abwesenheit.

Das Rauschen wird schließlich von einem großartigen Akkord unterbrochen, den ersten Tönen Eislers „Vom Sprengen des Gartens“, interpretiert von Heiner Goebbels im Jahr 2002.

Los Angeles mit seiner ausgebreiteten Skyline tritt orange und mit Smog verwaschen in Erscheinung, begleitet von einem gemächlichen Saxophonspiel. Aus dem Fenster eines fahrenden Zuges gefilmt führen uns Eberharts Aufnahmen durch ein industrielles Niemandsland am Rande der Stadt. In Untertiteln, die nicht gesprochen sind, einem wiederkehrenden Mittel dieses Films, lesen wir einen Auszug aus Eislers HUAC-Anhörungen, insbesondere die abschätzigen Kommentare des Vernehmers zu Eislers Werk: „Große Poesie, wie sie uns in Amerika gelehrt wird, hat nichts mit derartigem Müll zu tun.“

Eisler wiederum war enttäuscht von der kulturellen Landschaft Amerikas; zwar faszinierte ihn Hollywood, er lehnte aber dessen Mentalität ab. In einer späteren Sequenz des Films kehrt Eberhart zur ersten Einstellung des Plattenspielers zurück, wechselt aber alsbald zu im Biltmore Hotel gedrehten Szenen – sowohl ihrem eigenen

Material als auch zu Ausschnitten aus Hollywood-Filmen. Dies ist mit untertiteltem Text aus *Composing for the Films* überlagert, einem Buch, das 1947 von Eisler und Theodor W. Adorno als Analyse und Kritik an der Verwendung von Musik in der Filmindustrie geschrieben wurde.[4] Eisler hatte beobachtet, dass die meisten Regisseure von Musik lediglich erwarteten, dass sie die Geschehnisse auf der Leinwand untermale und das Publikum einlulle, also sein vollkommenes Eintauchen in den Film unterstütze. Die beiden Autoren plädierten stattdessen dafür, dass Musik sowohl die Künstlichkeit und Illusion des Mediums Film bewusstmache als auch einen eigenständigen Wert darstelle. Eisler sah in der Musik keinen ästhetischen Zweck, sondern in Anlehnung an Brechts dramatisches Werk den Transfer eines drängenden politischen Anliegens. Brechts Stücke zielen bekanntermaßen auf einen Verfremdungseffekt ab, der dem Publikum die Inszeniertheit der Aufführung vor Augen führen soll, etwa durch das Durchbrechen der sogenannten vierten Wand oder den unkonventionellen Einsatz von Licht und Musik. Diese „Verfremdung“ in der Kunst verdeutlicht, wie kulturelle Artefakte von ökonomischen und sozialen Mächten geformt werden und ermutigt das Publikum dazu, seine Vorstellungen und Glaubenssätze zu hinterfragen.

Ein gewisser Verfremdungseffekt lässt sich auch in Eberharts *Garten sprengen* erkennen. Obwohl der Film sowohl dem Ton als auch dem Bild größtmögliche Autonomie zugesteht, bilden sie dennoch ein Ganzes, das es fast unmöglich macht, sie getrennt voneinander zu betrachten. Das eine lenkt die Aufmerksamkeit auf das andere, oft durch die zeitweilige Abwesenheit von Ton oder Bild. Der Ton ist weder diegetisch (dem Bild entstammend) noch dekorativ. Ein sich wiederholender, von Eisler komponierter und von Eberhart modulierter Klavierakkord hält plötzlich inne, als das Bild zum Protagonisten wechselt, der auf den Hotelteppich springt, und vergegenwärtigt dem Publikum, dass es sich hierbei um eine technische Konstruktion handelt.

Indem sie das Verhältnis zwischen Bild und Ton aufbricht, hebt Eberhart auch die filmische Geste hervor. Der Protagonist des Films, gespielt vom Punkmusiker Ian F. Svenonius, erscheint als gesichtslose Gestalt, die durch die Räume des Hotels spukt: Er tanzt auf dem Teppich, streicht über das Holzfurnier, sieht aus dem Fenster, verschwindet im langen Korridor. Diese ruhigen Nahaufnahmen von kleinen Bewegungen – Svenonius' Körper im Zusammenspiel mit der Architektur – sind es, die Eberharts Film vorwärtstreiben, ohne dass es einer Handlung bedarf. In ihrem Essay über Brechts L.A.-Dichtung zitiert Quinn Latimer Lion Feuchtwangers Kommentar in einer BBC-Sendung von 1958: „Geschichte, Handlung, Kontinuität spielten keine Rolle für Brecht: Was ihm wichtig war, war die richtige Situation, die richtige Geste, das richtige Wort. Er visualisierte die Geste, aus der Geste entstand das Wort.“ In *Garten sprengen* führen uns Gesten in die Welt des Films und hin zu den weiteren Werken der Ausstellung. Mit ihrer Komposition von Bild und Ton befragt Eberhart die Konstruktion von Narrativen und setzt sie als Mittel zur Strukturierung gelebter Realität voraus. Die Filmwissenschaftlerin Christa Blümlinger stellt in ihrer Analyse der filmischen Geste fest: „Der Sinn einer Geste (an die Sprache gebunden) und ihrer Form (jenseits der Sprache) vollzieht sich im Zwischen, ein poetischer Raum zwischen dem Sichtbaren und dem Unsichtbaren, zwischen erkennbarem Muster und zarter Erscheinung.“[5] Diese Verschiebung von Plastizität zu Potenzialität trifft nicht nur auf Eberharts Film zu, sondern ebenso auf ihre im IKOB gezeigten skulpturalen und fotografischen Arbeiten.

Beim Betreten der Ausstellungsräume trifft man auf zwei Holzskulpturen, die der Filmleinwand gegenüberstehen und klassischen Klavierhockern ähneln. Auf einem

Objekt befindet sich eine Bleistiftzeichnung, die Eislers 10-inch Platte mit dem Titel „Rise Up“ nachempfunden ist. Diese hat er bei Timely Recording Company aufgenommen, einem New Yorker Label, das in den 1930er Jahren für die Veröffentlichung politischer Protestmusik bekannt war. Die beiden in Arbeitsanzügen gekleideten Figuren könnten gerade umfallen oder miteinander kämpfen, die Ambivalenz der Abbildung lässt verschiedene Interpretationen des Klassenkampfes und seiner Darstellung zu. Eine Skulptur an der Wand mit dem Titel *Book Holder & Pencil* (2023) besteht aus einer hölzernen Form, die einen vollständig aus Blei gegossenen Bleistift hält; das Buch selbst ist abwesend. Das Display der Filmleinwand ist hinten geöffnet und gibt die Trägerstruktur preis. Eine weitere Arbeit, *Eraser, Pencil, Pencil* (2023), ist halb versteckt hinter der Filmleinwand und innerhalb der Box platziert. Zwei Bleistifte, einer länger als der andere, lehnen an einem quaderförmigen Messingobjekt. Der beige Teppich, der den Boden bedeckt, erinnert an den Teppichboden des Biltmores – oder an die Wüste.

Eine Reihe von dreiundfünfzig Objekten aus Beton ist auf einem Podest im nächsten Raum platziert. Sie erinnern an die Pedale eines Klaviers, sind mit Pigmenten in verschiedenen Grautönen gegossen und stellen in Anlehnung an Eberharts Film eine Verbindung zwischen visueller und akustischer Wahrnehmung her. Eine analoge Fotografie an der Wand bietet einen Einblick in den ehemaligen Timely-Recording-Standort in der Fifth Avenue in Manhattan. Ähnlich wie das Biltmore Hotel in *Garten sprengen* positioniert Eberhart das Gebäude als eine Protagonistin der Geschichte, eine architektonische Zeugin dessen, was hinter seiner Fassade geschehen ist. *Fold* (2023), eine weitere Holzskulptur auf dem Boden des Ausstellungsraumes, besteht aus zwei schräg angeordneten, leicht über dem Boden schwebenden, Klavierdeckeln ähnelnden Formen. Die beiden Teile werden durch einen leicht gebogenen, dünnen Stab gestützt und voneinander getrennt, was die Zerbrechlichkeit des Objekts betont. Wie zwei sich im Schließen befindende Buchdeckel, oder die beiden Arbeiter in Eberharts Zeichnung, spielt die Spannung zwischen den beiden Elementen mit den Erwartungen der Betrachtenden – vielleicht eine materialisierte Interpretation von Eislers Kompositionen.

Stille ist beunruhigend ebenso wie Leere. Veronika Eberharts Werk spricht von einem Verständnis des Wesentlichen, das ohne das Zufällige nicht existieren kann. Die Pausen in *Garten sprengen* sind niemals absolut. Das Rauschen des Plattenspielers, das Zögern und nervöse Hantieren bei den HUAC-Anhörungen sprechen von den bewegten Biografien, die den Film durchziehen und vom unbehaglichen Schweigen der Zensur.

Der letzte Teil der Ausstellung im IKOB erstreckt sich in jene Räume des Museums, die normalerweise für Besucher·innen nicht zugänglich sind. Im Korridor zum Büro hängt eine Serie von Fotografien der Schallplatten, die Eisler mit Timely produziert hat. Diese Zusammenarbeit wurde später zum Gegenstand von Eislers HUAC-Anhörungen und trug zu seiner Ausweisung aus den Vereinigten Staaten bei. Eberhart erhielt in verschiedenen US-amerikanischen Archiven Zugang zu diesen Platten. Einige ihrer Kanten sind abgeschlagen, aber die Etiketten sind intakt. Sie tragen jeweils eine Zeichnung und den Titel der Platte, darunter das bereits erwähnte „Rise Up“ sowie „In Praise of Learning“, „United Front“ und „The Soup Song“. Unterhalb der aufgereihten Fotografien stehen Regale mit Archivboxen des Museums. Indem sie die vierte Wand der Ausstellungsräumlichkeiten aufbricht und das Publikum zum Betreten auffordert, lenkt Eberhart die Aufmerksamkeit auf Fragen der Kunst, des Zugangs und des kulturellen Gedächtnisses: Welche Kunstwerke werden bewahrt, in Erinnerung behalten, beachtet? Warum und wie lange?

Zensur hat die Macht, Dinge verschwinden zu lassen oder sie umso sichtbarer zu machen. Bei der Begegnung mit diesen Fotografien im Museumsbüro scheint es so, als würden beide Zustände – Abwesenheit und Anwesenheit – auf Eislers Schallplatten zutreffen.

Jennifer Egans 2011 erschienenes Buch *A Visit from the Goon Squad*[6] ist eine Sammlung von dreizehn Geschichten, die alle in der Rockmusik-Branche spielen. Ein Kapitel kommt in Form einer tagebuchartigen PowerPoint-Präsentation daher, erstellt von der Teenagerin Alison. Ihr Bruder Lincoln ist „besessen von Rocksongs, die Pausen enthalten." Alisons Folien erzählen nicht nur vom Familienleben in der kalifornischen Wüste, sie schildern auch die minutiösen Beobachtungen, die ihr Bruder über die jeweiligen Pausen anstellt: ihr Timing, ihre Länge und ihre möglichen Interpretationen. Lincoln wirft David Bowie beispielsweise vor, sich „davor gedrückt" zu haben, eine Pause in „Young Americans" auf eine ganze Sekunde auszudehnen, oder verweist darauf, dass man in „Foxy Lady" während einer zwei Sekunden langen Pause Jimi Hendrix atmen hören kann. Er liebt es, die Pausen im Loop abzuspielen, sodass sie minutenlang andauern. Alison zählt die Dinge auf, die ihr während der geloopten Pausen auffallen: „ein Hauch von Orange am Horizont"; „Tausend schwarze Turbinen"; „Man gewöhnt sich nie an die Sterne, egal, wie lange man hier lebt." Die Pausen sind nicht bloße Abwesenheit, sie ermöglichen es vielmehr, dass andere Dinge geschehen können.

> *Die Pause lässt einen glauben, dass das Lied zu Ende ist. Und dann ist der Song gar nicht richtig zu Ende, deshalb ist man erleichtert. Aber dann endet er doch, denn jedes Lied hat natürlich ein Ende, und DIESMAL – IST – ENDGÜLTIG – ALLES – VORBEI.*

Einmal gehen Alison und ihr Vater in die Wüste hinaus. Die Wüste ist still und laut zugleich und Alison hört in der Leere ein Klicken und Summen. „Die ganze Wüste ist eine Pause", bemerkt sie. Es sind die Pausen, die die Wahrheit über Musik, das Erleben von Kunst und das Leben auf dieser Welt erzählen. Dieser Gedanke trifft auch auf Veronika Eberharts Werk und ihren nuancierten Gebrauch von Rhythmus zu, der sich nicht nur aus den tatsächlichen Tönen der Musik erschafft, sondern vor allem aus den Lücken dazwischen. Leere und Stille sind entscheidend für ihren Montageprozess und erzeugen eine vielfältige Präsenz.

Wenn der Abspann von Eberharts Kinofassung des Films[7] zu laufen beginnt, setzt Eislers vollständige Wiedergabe vom „Sprengen des Gartens" aus den „Hollywoodelegien" ein. Eisler singt zuerst so beiläufig, als würde er von seinem Tag erzählen, und steigert sich dann zu einem Art Manifest, einer Elegie für die Unterschicht des Grüns:

> *Vergiß nicht das Strauchwerk, auch*
> *Das beerenlose nicht, das ermattete*
> *Und übersieh mir nicht*
> *Zwischen den Blumen das Unkraut, das auch*
> *Durst hat. Noch gieße nur*
> *Den frischen Rasen oder den versengten nur:*
> *Auch den nackten Boden erfrische du.*

Brecht und Eisler fühlten sich wahrscheinlich, ebenso wie die anderen im Exil, gleich dem Unkraut von Los Angeles, das in einer ihm feindlich gesinnten Umgebung Wurzeln schlägt, in der Sonne brennt und nach Wasser durstet. Latimer schreibt treffend: „Brecht schien sein Augenmerk stets auf Fundamente zu legen – seien sie natürlich oder politisch – und die Weise, in der sie jederzeit zerbröckeln können." „Vom Sprengen des Gartens" holt nicht nur die unterprivilegierten Bewohner·innen pflegeintensiver Gärten vor den Vorhang, sondern thematisiert auch die Abwesenheit erkennbaren Lebens. Das, was für Brecht und Eisler die eigentliche Landschaft von Los Angeles war: kahle Erde, Wüste, alles, was darauf gebaut ist, eine Illusion.

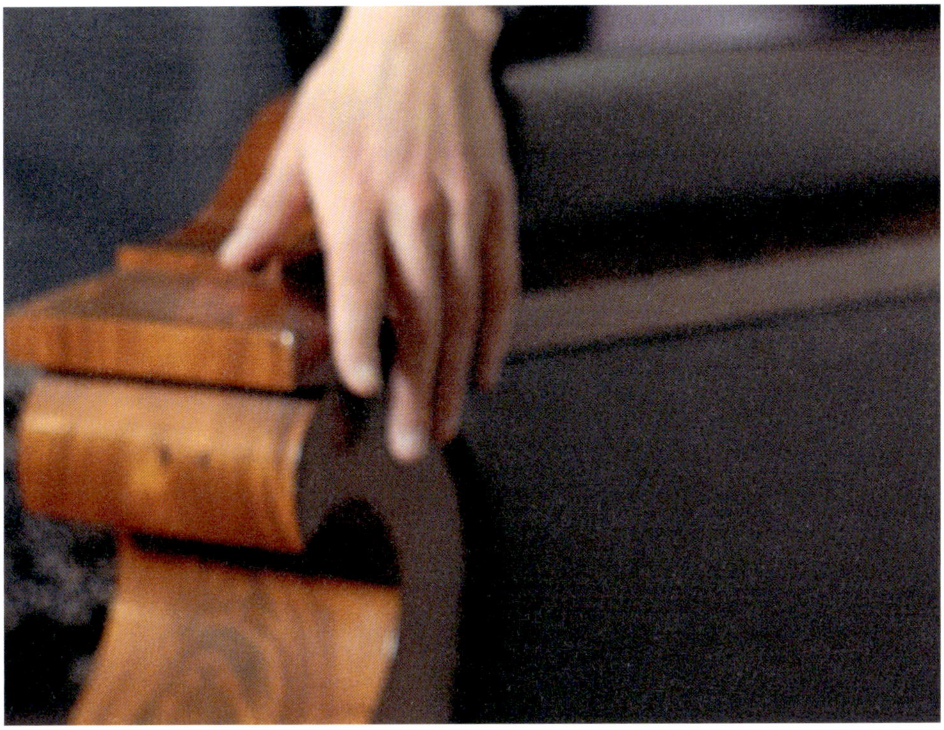

The whole desert is a pause

Brenda Guesnet

1 Quinn Latimer, "Kalifornien träumen: Bertolt Brecht's LA Poetry, and Other Sunstruck Germanic Specters," in: *Like a Woman: Essays, Readings, Poems*, Berlin / London: Sternberg Press, 2017, p. 27.

2 For example, "Solidaritätslied" ("Solidarity Song," 1931) and "Einheitsfrontlied" ("United Front Song," 1934), both with lyrics by Brecht, were catchy sing-along anthems for the working-class movement.

3 See Mike Davis, *City of Quartz: Excavating the Future in Los Angeles*, London / New York: Verso Books, 1990.

4 Theodor Adorno, Hanns Eisler, *Composing for the Films*, New York: Oxford University Press, 1947.

5 Christa Blümlinger, "The Filmed Body and the Cinematic Gesture: Zoe Beloff's Revisions," in: *European Journal of Media Studies*, NECSUS 8 (2), Autumn 2019: 169–188 URL: https://necsus-ejms.org/

6 Jennifer Egan, "Great Rock and Roll Pauses by Alison Blake", in: *A Visit from the Goon Squad*, New York: Knopf, 2010.

7 There are two versions of the film *Garten sprengen*, one for cinemas, complete with end credits, and another for exhibition contexts that does not include the credits as it is continuously looped.

"Garten sprengen"
in German is an ambiguous phrase, open to nuanced interpretation: I hear it as *exploding* the garden, while it could also be read as *watering* the garden. The title of Veronika Eberhart's film and eponymous exhibition at IKOB Museum of Contemporary Art, Belgium draws from the 1942 poem "Vom Sprengen des Gartens" by Bertolt Brecht, which he wrote with the composer Hanns Eisler in mind, for their "Hollywood Elegies:"

> *O Sprengen des Gartens, das Grün zu ermutigen!*
> *Wässern der durstigen Bäume! Gib mehr als genug.*
>
> *Oh watering of the garden to encourage the greenery!*
> *Watering of the thirsty trees! Give more than enough.*

At the time Brecht wrote these lines, he was living in exile in Los Angeles, and the greenery surrounding him was of concern. The city struck him with numerous metaphors of its apparent contradictions: he was at once delighted and disturbed to see so many parks and gardens, all in need of copious amounts of water and expensive irrigation systems to stay alive in the middle of the desert. Like the plants, Brecht himself was an unlikely resident of Los Angeles, along with many other German-speaking exiles (Hanns Eisler, Peter Lorre, Fritz Lang, Theodor W. Adorno, Salka Viertel, Arnold Schoenberg and Heinrich Mann among them). Members of the European avant-garde, who, in the words of American writer Quinn Latimer, "fled the killing fields of World War II Europe and found themselves in a city of angels nestled along the cerulean pool of the Pacific."[1]

Brecht's most important collaborator at this time was the German-Austrian composer Hanns Eisler (1898–1962). The two met in 1930, and Eisler subsequently composed the music for many of Brecht's texts and plays. As a staunch Marxist, Eisler considered music a powerful tool to express and disseminate the socialist worldview to mass audiences. Combining elements of popular and classical music in his compositions, he made music for the working class, for political engagement, and for the mobilization of revolution. Text and music were valued as complementary, effectively imparting political messages.[2]

Eisler immigrated to the United States in 1938 after the situation for Jews and left-wing artists in his native Austria and Germany had become untenable. Brecht followed in 1941. Brecht and Eisler continued their friendship and collaboration in Los Angeles, most notably on the 1943 film *Hangmen also Die!* directed by Fritz Lang. Eisler was nominated for an Academy Award for his score, and the success of these exiled German native speakers testifies to the influence of their work on American culture. However, it wasn't long before Eisler's political views began to cause him trouble in his adopted home country. He and many other European intellectuals were under constant surveillance from the FBI, and the scrutiny only intensified in the following years. In 1947, Eisler was interrogated by the House Un-American Activities Committee (HUAC) and was accused of acting as a Soviet agent. One year later, he was expelled from the country, returning to Vienna, and later settling in the GDR. Here he composed "Auferstanden aus Ruinen" ("Risen from Ruins," 1949), which became the national anthem of the young republic.

Veronika Eberhart's 2022 film *Garten sprengen* is set at the location where Eisler's first secret HUAC hearings took place: the Biltmore Hotel in Los Angeles. Eleven stories high and taking up half of a city block, its various ballrooms have been the setting for Hollywood films and Academy Awards ceremonies. Pointing her 16mm camera at the hotel's cascading staircases, elaborately patterned carpets, and sprawling dining halls, the symbolic specificity of the Biltmore allows Eberhart to connect the broader themes surrounding Eisler's biography with the realm of the dream factory. Los Angeles, the master of urban dialectic, of sunshine and noir, as Mike Davis would describe it,[3] is interwoven with notions of being in exile and the threat of censorship. Coupling an interior gaze with a sprawling investigative outlook is an approach often employed by Eberhart. Her work interprets specific historical references, merging rigorous research and poetic impressions into complex arrangements of artistic expression encompassing video, sculpture, and installation. Ranging from Goethe's *Faust,* to Lacanian epiphanies in Baltimore, to her fascination with Eisler, she skillfully utilizes her sources into potent meditations on art history, politics, and society. While her works are frequently rooted in specific places, their sense of time remains ambiguous.

Garten sprengen explores the still functioning Biltmore Hotel as a site of cultural production: both its highly public, televised stage presence as well as its functioning as the location for top secret hearings, shielded and hidden from the public eye. Sampled footage includes the hotel room scenes from *Beverly Hills Cop* (1984) and *I Wanna Hold Your Hand* (1978) among filmed excerpts from Brecht and Eisler's HUAC hearings (1947). We come to understand all these events as integral to the administration of what is permissible in cultural expression and what is not. In the first shot, someone puts on a record, but all one hears is static. It foreshadows a central point of this remarkable 12-minute film: the significance of silence, of pauses, of absence.

The white noise is interrupted by a gorgeous, earthy chord, the first notes of Eisler's "Vom Sprengen des Gartens," interpreted by Heiner Goebbels in 2002. The sprawling skyline of Los Angeles comes into view, orange and fuzzy with pollution. Filmed from the window of a moving train, Eberhart's images take us across an industrial no man's land on the outskirts of the city, accompanied by an unhurried saxophone. In subtitles that are not spoken, a recurring device of this film, we read an extract from Eisler's HUAC hearings and in particular the disparaging comments of the interviewer: "Great poetry as we are taught in America, has nothing to do with that kind of truck," referring to Eisler's work.

Eisler, in turn, was dismayed by the cultural landscape of America, fascinated by Hollywood but rejecting its modus operandi. In a later sequence of *Garten sprengen*, Eberhart returns to the opening shot of the record player and cuts to scenes filmed in the Biltmore Hotel – her own material as well as samples from Hollywood films. This is overlaid with subtitled text extracted from *Composing for the Films*, a book written by Eisler and Theodor W. Adorno in 1947 as an analysis and critique of the treatment of music in the film industry.[4] Eisler observed that most directors wanted music to simply reflect what is happening on the screen, coddling the viewer. Sound is prescribed a prosthetic function to support one's full immersion in the film. The authors argued instead that music should both make us aware of the artifice and the illusion of the medium of film, and function autonomously. For Eisler this was not an aesthetic preference, but an urgent political matter in alignment with Brecht's theater work, which sought to achieve a so-called *Verfremdungseffekt* (alienation effect) – a reminder to the audience that they are watching a staged performance through the breaking of the fourth wall and unconventional use of lighting and music. The idea was that this "defamiliarization" in art would reveal how cultural artifacts are shaped by economic and social forces, and thereby encourage the audience to question their assumptions and beliefs.

One can identify a kind of *Verfremdungseffekt* in Eberhart's *Garten sprengen*. While the film grants autonomy to both its sound and visuals, they also create a whole that makes it almost impossible to imagine them separately. One draws attention to the other, often through the intermittent absence of either sound or image. The sound is never diegetic (occurring "on screen"), yet it isn't ornamental either. A repeating piano chord written by Eisler and modulated by Eberhart pauses suddenly when the image switches to the protagonist jumping on the hotel's carpet, making the viewer aware they are watching a technical construction.

In destabilizing the relationship between image and sound, Eberhart also places emphasis on the cinematic gesture. The film's protagonist, played by punk musician Ian F. Svenonius, appears as a faceless figure haunting the rooms of the hotel: he dances on the carpet, strokes the wooden veneer, gazes out the window, disappears into the long corridors. These lingering close-ups of small movements – Svenonius' body interacting with the architecture – are what drives Eberhart's film forward, without the need for a storyline or plot. In her essay on Brecht's LA poetry, Latimer quotes Lion Feuchtwanger's comments from a 1958 BBC program: "story, plot, continuity did not matter to [Brecht]: what mattered to him was the right situation, the right gesture, the right word. He visualized the gesture, out from the gesture grew the word." In *Garten sprengen*, gestures lead us into the world of the film and towards the larger body of work surrounding it. Eberhart questions the construction of narrative with her composition of image and sound, positing them as instruments used to structure lived reality. Film scholar Christa Blümlinger, in her analysis of the cinematic gesture, states: "The sense of gesture (linked to language) and its form (beyond language) is realized in the space *in-between*, a poetic space between the visible and the invisible, between an intelligible pattern and tenuous appearance."[5] This shift from plasticity to potentiality applies not only to Eberhart's film but is also crucial to her sculptural and photographic works presented at IKOB.

On entering the exhibition space, one encounters two wooden sculptures facing the film screen and resembling classical piano stools. A pencil drawing on one of the stools is based on the label of one of Eisler's 10-inch records titled "Rise Up," recorded with New York-based Timely Recording, known for releasing political protest music in the 1930s. The two figures dressed in workers' overalls could be tumbling down or fighting one another, the ambivalence of the composition leaves open different interpretations of class struggle and its representation. On the wall, a sculpture entitled *Book Holder & Pencil* (2023) consists of a wooden form that holds a pencil, cast entirely in lead; the book itself is absent. The display-box for the film screen is open at the back, revealing its support structure. Another work, *Eraser, Pencil, Pencil* (2023) is half-hidden behind the film screen and positioned within the frame of the box. Two lead pencils, one longer than the other, lean against a rectangular brass object. The beige carpet covering the floor recalls the carpeting of the Biltmore, or even indeed the desert.

A row of fifty-three objects in concrete are laid out on a pedestal in the next room. Reminiscent of the pedals of a piano, they are cast with pigments of varying shades of gray, echoing Eberhart's film in the way they create a connection between visual and sonic perception. An analog photograph on the wall offers a glimpse into the former office of Timely Recording on Fifth Avenue in Manhattan. Similar to the Biltmore Hotel in *Garten sprengen*, Eberhart positions the building as a protagonist of history, an architectural witness to what happened behind its façade. On the exhibition floor, another wooden sculpture, *Fold (2023)*, consists of two piano lid-like shapes arranged at an angle and seemingly hovering above the ground. The two parts are separated and propped up by a slightly bent, thin rod reinforcing the object's fragility. Like two book flaps about to close – or the two workers in Eberhart's drawing – the tension between the two elements plays with the viewer's expectations, maybe a materialized interpretation of Eisler's compositions.

Silence is unsettling, as is emptiness. Veronika Eberhart's work speaks to an understanding that the integral cannot exist without the incidental. The pauses in *Garten sprengen* are never absolute. The white noise of the record player, the hesitations and nervous fiddling in the HUAC hearings all speak to the troubled biographies the film is inhabiting, and the uneasy silence of censorship.

The final part of the exhibition at IKOB extends into the museum's rooms that are normally inaccessible to visitors. In the office corridor hangs a series of photographs of the records Eisler produced with Timely Recording. The collaboration later became the subject of Eisler's HUAC hearings and contributed to his expulsion from the United States. Eberhart gained access to these records in various archives in the USA. Some of their edges are chipped but the labels are intact, each bearing a drawing and the name of the record, including the aforementioned "Rise Up," as well as "In Praise Of Learning," "United Front," and "The Soup Song." Below the row of photographs, visitors encounter shelves filled with the museum's archival boxes. By breaking the fourth wall of the exhibition space and encouraging the audience to trespass, Eberhart calls attention to questions of art, access, and cultural memory: what art works are kept, remembered, paid attention to? Why, and for how long? Censorship has the power to make things disappear or to make them all the more visible. Encountering these photographs in the museum's offices, it seems as if both states – absence and presence – are true in regard to Eisler's records.

Jennifer Egan's 2011 novel *A Visit from the Goon Squad*[6] is a collection of thirteen stories, all of them set in and around the rock music business. One chapter is written entirely in the form of a diaristic PowerPoint presentation, put together by Alison, a teenage character. Her brother Lincoln is "obsessed with rock songs that have pauses in them," and Alison's slides capture their family life in the Californian desert alongside his minute observations about these pauses: their timing, length, and his interpretation of them. Lincoln accuses David Bowie of "chickening out" by not extending a pause in "Young Americans" to a full second, and points out that in "Foxy Lady," you can hear Jimi Hendrix breathing during a two-second pause. He enjoys looping the pauses so that they last for minutes. Alison lists the things she notices during the looped pauses: "a whisper of orange on the horizon," "a thousand black turbines," "you can't get used to the stars, no matter how long you live here." The pauses are not simply the absence of music, they allow for other things to happen.

> *The pause makes you think the song will end. And then the song isn't really over, so you're relieved. But then the song does actually end, because every song ends, obviously, and THAT. TIME. THE. END. IS. FOR. REAL.*

At one point, Alison and her father walk out into the desert. The desert is silent and loud at the same time, and Alison hears clicks and hums in the emptiness. "The whole desert is a pause," she observes. It is the pauses that tell the truth about music, experiencing art, and being alive in this world. This thought also applies to Veronika Eberhart's work and her nuanced use of rhythm, depending not only on the actual tones of music but especially on the gaps in-between. Emptiness and silence are crucial to her process of montage, evoking a spectral presence.

When the end credits of Eberhart's cinematic version of the film[7] begin, Eisler's full rendition of "Vom Sprengen des Gartens" from the "Hollywood Elegies" sets in. Eisler sings it first off-handedly, as if telling you about his day, then crescendoing to a manifesto of sorts, an elegy for the underclass of greenery:

> *Vergiß nicht das Strauchwerk, auch*
> *Das beerenlose nicht, das ermattete*
> *Und übersieh mir nicht*
> *Zwischen den Blumen das Unkraut, das auch*
> *Durst hat. Noch gieße nur*
> *Den frischen Rasen oder den versengten nur:*
> *Auch den nackten Boden erfrische du.*

Do not forget the bushes, even
Those without any berries, the drooping
ones! And do not overlook
The weeds between the flowers that are also
Thirsty. Also do not water only the fresh lawn, or the singed lawn:
Refresh even the naked soil.

Brecht and Eisler, along with their fellow exiles, likely felt an affinity with the weeds of Los Angeles, taking root in an environment hostile to their presence, baking in the sun and thirsting to be watered. Latimer aptly writes: "Brecht appeared to be forever alert to foundations – be they natural or political – and the way they could crumble at a moment's notice." "Vom Sprengen des Gartens" calls attention not only to the underprivileged inhabitants of high-maintenance gardens, but to the absence of discernible life. What Brecht and Eisler saw as the real landscape of Los Angeles: bare soil, the desert, everything built on top of it a mirage.

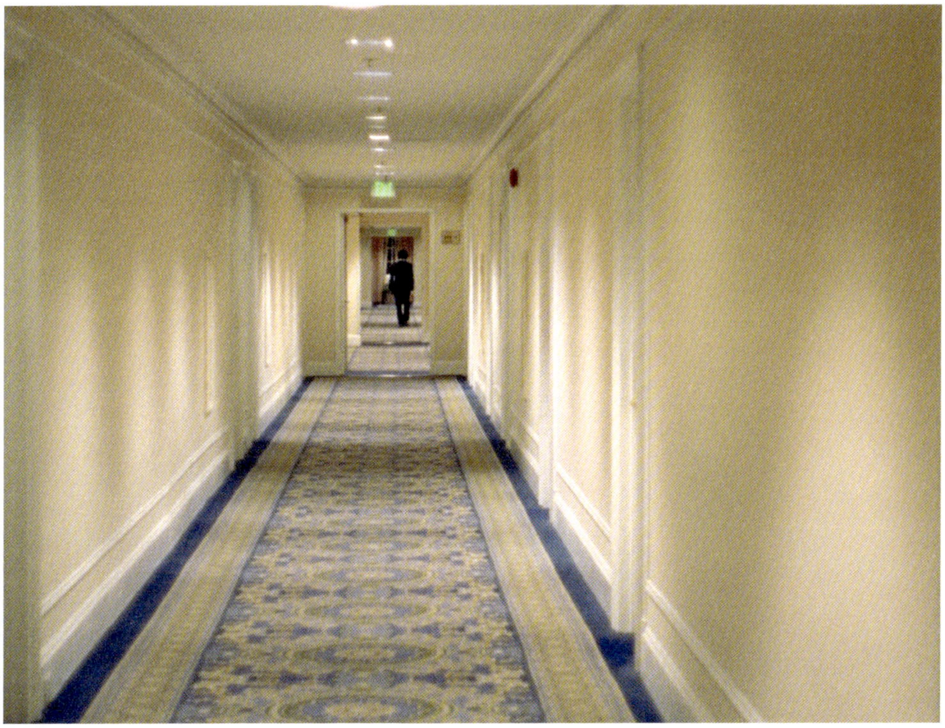

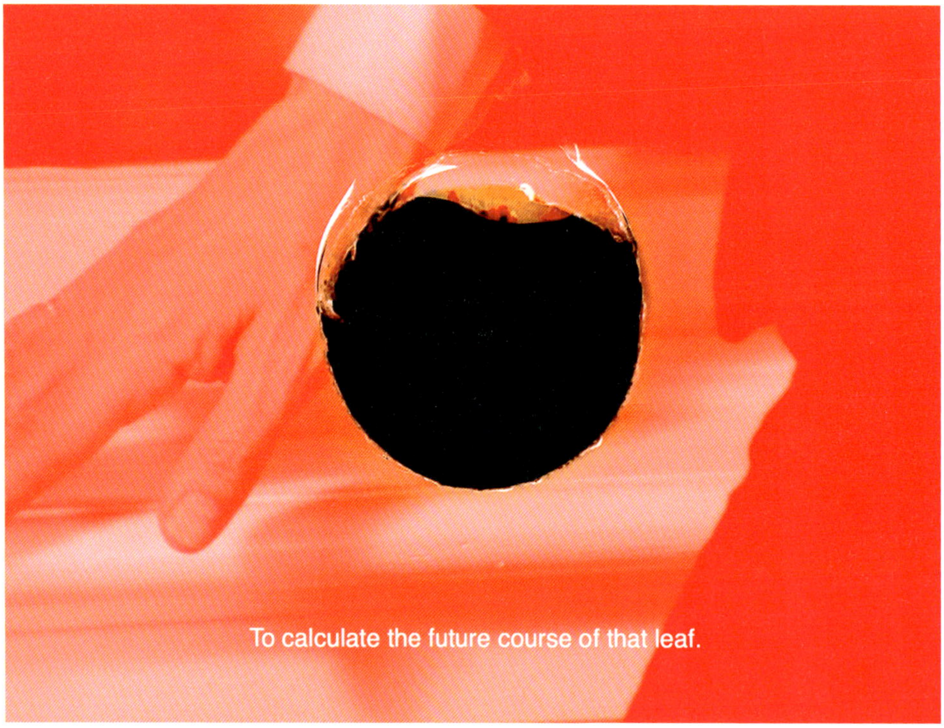
To calculate the future course of that leaf.

Garten sprengen, 2022
16mm Film übertragen auf|
transferred to HD, 12 min

Regie | Director
Veronika Eberhart

Performer Hotel
Ian F. Svenonius

Performer Hand
Friedel Schmoranzer

Kamera | Cinematography
Chloe Reyes at Biltmore Hotel &
Los Angeles Central Library

Veronika Eberhart at KINGDOM
DAY PARADE LOS ANGELES,
Villa Aurora, USC Special
Collections, Special Research
Collections University of
California, Santa Barbara

Schnitt | Editing
Veronika Eberhart

Sound Design
Veronika Eberhart

Musik | Music
"Vom Sprengen des Gartens",
Heiner Goebbels: Eislermaterial
Performed by Josef Bierbichler,
Ensemble Modern
Courtesy of ECM Records, ECM
New Series

"Vom Sprengen des Gartens",
Die Hollywood-Elegien
Performed by Hanns Eisler
Courtesy of BREITKOPF &
HAERTEL KG

Tonmischung | Re-recording
mixer
Andreas Pils

Tonrestaurierung | Audio
restauration
Katrin Euller

Farbkorrekur | Color correction
Matthias Halibrand,
Patrick Weber

Zitate | Quotes
*Johannes (Hanns) Eisler appears
before a Subcommittee of the House
Un-American Activities Committee,
in Los Angeles*, California at
the Biltmore Hotel, 1947, May 12

I Wanna Hold Your Hand, 1978

Beverly Hills Cop, 1984

*Bertolt Brecht before the Committee
on Un-American Activities*, 1947

*Hanns Eisler before the Committee
on Un-American Activities*, 1947

*Composing for the Films by Hanns
Eisler and Theodor W. Adorno*, 1947

Bertolt Brecht, *Autumn in
California*, 1945

BRENDA GUESNET ist Kuratorin und Autorin. Sie arbeitet seit 2021 als Kuratorin und stellvertretende Direktorin im IKOB – Museum für Zeitgenössische Kunst in Eupen, in der Deutschsprachigen Gemeinschaft Belgiens. Seit 2015 realisiert sie unabhängige kuratorische Projekte, sie ist zudem Mitinitiatorin von celador, einem 2023 gegründeten Projektraum in Brüssel. Zuvor arbeitete sie in der Artist Liaison Abteilung von White Cube, London (2017–2020), nachdem sie einen MFA in Curating am Goldsmiths College, University of London (2015–17) absolvierte.

BRENDA GUESNET is a curator and writer. Since 2021, she has been Curator and Deputy Director at IKOB – Museum of Contemporary Art in Eupen, in the German-speaking community of Belgium. She has worked on independent curatorial projects since 2015, and was a co-initiator of celador, a project space in Brussels founded in 2023. Previously, she worked in the Artist Liaison department at White Cube, London (2017–2020), after completing an MFA in Curating at Goldsmiths, University of London (2015–2017).

KEVIN VENNEMANN lehrt am Scripps College in Claremont, Kalifornien, und lebt in Los Angeles. Zuletzt erschien bei Matthes & Seitz Berlin die Studie *Die Welt vom Rücken des Kranichs. Thermodynamik und der Verfall einer Familie* (2020), zuvor der Essay *Sunset Boulevard. Vom Filmen, Bauen und Sterben in Los Angeles* (Suhrkamp Verlag, 2012).

KEVIN VENNEMANN teaches at Scripps College in Claremont, California, and lives in Los Angeles. His most recent publications include *Die Welt vom Rücken des Kranichs. Thermodynamik und der Verfall einer Familie* (Matthes & Seitz Berlin, 2020), and *Sunset Boulevard. Vom Filmen, Bauen und Sterben in Los Angeles* (Suhrkamp Verlag, 2012).

IAN F. SVENONIUS ist der Autor der Bücher *Against the Written Word* (2023), *Censorship Now!!* (2015), *Supernatural Strategies for Making a Rock 'n' Roll Group* (2013) und *The Psychic Soviet* (2006), alle erschienen bei Akashic Books, New York. Er war Gastgeber der VBS.tv-Sendung Soft Focus, in der er unter anderem Mark E. Smith, Genesis P-Orridge, Chan Marshall und Ian MacKaye interviewte. Als Musiker hat er mehr als zwanzig Alben und unzählige Singles in verschiedenen Rock'n'Roll-Kombinationen (Escape-ism, Chain & the Gang, The Make-Up, The Nation of Ulysses usw.) veröffentlicht. Er lebt in Los Angeles, CA.

IAN F. SVENONIUS is the author of *Against the Written Word* (2023), *Censorship Now!!* (2015), *Supernatural Strategies for Making a Rock 'n' Roll Group* (2013) and *The Psychic Soviet* (2006), all published by Akashic Books, New York. He was the host of VBS.tv's Soft Focus, where he interviewed Mark E. Smith, Genesis P-Orridge, Chan Marshall, and Ian MacKaye, among others. He has released more than twenty albums and countless singles in various rock'n'roll groups (Escape-ism, Chain & the Gang, The Make-Up, The Nation of Ulysses, etc.). He lives in Los Angeles, CA.

VERONIKA EBERHART, geboren in Bad Radkersburg, Österreich, ist Künstlerin und Musikerin. Ihr Schaffen bewegt sich in einem breiten Spektrum zwischen Film, Sound, Performance, Fotografie, Skulptur und Installation. Eberharts Praxis zeichnet sich durch eine hohe Musikalität, als auch durch die Verhandlung konzeptueller Fragestellungen zu räumlichen Metaphern aus. Ihre Recherche zu Hanns Eislers Exiljahren begann, als sie 2019 das Schindler-Stipendium am MAK Center for Art and Architecture in Los Angeles erhielt.

VERONIKA EBERHART, born in Bad Radkersburg, Austria, is an artist and musician. She holds an MFA in Visual Arts from the Academy of Fine Arts Vienna, and an MA in Sociology from the University of Vienna. Eberhart works conceptually across the fields of film, sculpture, performance, sound, photography, and spatial installations. Her use of media is distinguished both by its high musicality and the negotiation of conceptual issues that challenge hierarchical spatial metaphors. Her research on Hanns Eisler's years of exile began when she was the recipient of the Schindler Scholarship from the MAK Center for Art and Architecture in Los Angeles in 2019.

Book Holder & Pencil, 2023
Holz, Blei | Wood, Lead
20 × 15 × 3 cm

S. | p. 49

Ausstellungsansicht | Exhibition view

S. | pp. 50–57

Eraser, Pencil, Pencil, 2023
Messing, Pigment, Blei | Brass, Pigment, Lead
Größe variabel | dimensions variable

S. | p. 58

Sit Down, Rise Up II, 2023
Holz, Bleistiftzeichnung | Wood, Pencil-Drawing
65 × 55 × 30 cm

S. | p. 61

Detailansicht | Detail, *Sit Down, Rise Up II*, 2023

S. | p. 63

Ausstellungsansicht | Exhibition view

S. | pp. 64–65

235 5th Avenue I, 2023
Inkjet Print
27,5 × 38 × 3 cm

S. | p. 67

235 5th Avenue II, 2023
Inkjet Print
27,5 × 38 × 3 cm

S. | p. 68

235 5th Avenue III, 2023
Inkjet Print
27,5 × 38 × 3 cm

S. | p. 69

Detailansicht | Detail, *Untitled (53 Pedals)*, 2023
Beton, Pigment | Concrete, Pigment
Größe variabel | dimensions variable

S. | p. 71

Ausstellungsansicht | Exhibition view

S. | pp. 72–73

Detailansicht | Detail, *Untitled (53 Pedals)*, 2023

S. | pp. 74–75

Fold, 2023
Holz, Schrauben | Wood, Screws
95 × 105 × 95 cm

S. | pp. 76–77

Ausstellungsansicht | Exhibition view

S. | pp. 78–79

Rise Up, Timely (Chipped), 2023
Inkjet Print
38 × 38 × 3cm

S. | p. 81

In Praise Of Learning, Timely (Chipped), 2023
Inkjet Print
38 × 38 × 3 cm

S. | p. 83

United Front, Timely, 2023
Inkjet Print
38 × 38 × 3 cm

S. | p. 85

The Soup Song, Timely, 2023
Inkjet Print
38 × 38 × 3 cm

S. | p. 87

Rise Up

In Praise of Learning

United Front

The Soup Song

Die Künstlerin dankt | The artist would like to thank Brenda Guesnet für ihren Enthusiasmus und ihr Vertrauen | for her enthusiasm and trust; dem gesamten Team des IKOB – Museum für Zeitgenössische Kunst für die tolle Unterstützung | the whole Team of IKOB – Museum of Contemporary Art for the great support; Phileas – The Austrian Office for Contemporary Art, insbesondere | particularly Jasper Sharp, Margherita Belcredi & Anna Hugo für die Großzügigkeit | for their generosity; Marie Artaker für ihre Expertise und ihre Geduld | for her expertise and patience; Kevin Vennemann & Ian F. Svenonius für die exzellenten Beiträge | for their excellent contributions; Gianna Virginia Prein, Eleanor Taylor, Michael Azerrad & Andreas Dvořák für ihre Genauigkeit und konstruktiven Vorschläge | for their accuracy and constructive suggestions; Klemens Waldhuber, Markus Tschiggerl & Patrick Anthofer für die Assistenz in der Ausstellungsproduktion | for the assistance of the exhibition production; Stefan Pedersen & Kevin Dooley für den kollektiven Prozess der Bildanalyse | for engaging in a collective process of image analyses; Florian Regl & Patrick Anthofer für die Präzision | for their precision; Michaela Ullmann & USC Special, David Seibert & Collections & Special Research Collections University of California, Santa Barbara; Pierre Crépon für das Teilen seiner Quellen und Recherche | for sharing resources and research; Heiner Goebbels, Chloe Reyes, Cordula Thym, Miriam Stoney, Theodor Maier, Renate Messenbäck, Arturo Silva, Nicholas Hoffman, Kathi Hofer, Eva Engelbert, Katrin Euller, Matthias Halibrand, Echo Park Film Center, Friedel Schmoranzer, Eva Seiler, Jule Saupe, Anna Schachinger, Victoria Langmann, Juliane Bischoff, Vincent Solange K. Stroep, Erna Eberhart, Alois Eberhart, Ruth Eberhart, Claudia Slanar, Sixpackfilm, Spector Books, Vanessa Joan Müller, Sebastian Höglinger, Peter Schernhuber, Andreas Pils, Lola Pertsowsky, Esther Lin, Stephanie Stern, Patrick Weber, Johanna Thorell, Siegfried Füreder, Saša Stanojević, Almut Reichenbach, Hannes Fauland, Paula Marschalek, Christian Egger, school – Performative Screenings, Willem Oorebeek, Simon Thompson, Sylvie Eyberg, Vinylograph, Natascha Muhić, Georg Mayr, Christopher Hütmannsberger, Waltraud Strommer & Österreichisches Kulturforum Brüssel, Anne König, Jan Wenzel, MAK Center for Art and Architecture in Los Angeles.

This book is published on the occasion of the exhibition

Veronika Eberhart: Garten sprengen

IKOB – Museum of Contemporary Art, Eupen, Belgium
Rotenberg 12/B
4700 Eupen, BEL
www.ikob.be

December 12, 2023 – March 10, 2024

This project was produced in collaboration with
Phileas – The Austrian Office for Contemporary Art

Curator
Brenda Guesnet

Editor
IKOB – Museum of Contemporary Art & Veronika Eberhart

Book design
Marie Artaker

Texts
Kevin Vennemann
Veronika Eberhart
Ian F. Svenonius
Brenda Guesnet

Copy editing
Renate Messenbäck
Arturo Silva

Proofreading
Anne König
Georg Mayr
Christopher Hütmannsberger

Translations
Miriam Stoney
Theodor Maier

Additional eye
Gianna Virginia Prein
Eleanor Taylor
Michael Azerrad
Andreas Dvořák
Stefan Pedersen

Image editing
Florian Regl

Additional image editing:
Phonograph Records
Patrick Anthofer

IKOB Team
Charlotte Bohn
Serge Cloot
Brenda Guesnet
Frank-Thorsten Moll
Ingrid Mossoux
Aida Willemen
Wouter Huis

Image credits
Lola Pertsowsky:
Exhibition views

Veronika Eberhart:
Film stills *Garten sprengen*, 2022
Carr & Driver, 2021
pp. 28–29

Printing
Gerin, Wolkersdorf

Paper
Munken Pure, 300 g/m²
GardaPat 13 KIARA, 135 g/m²

Typeface
Timez (La Bolde Vita)

Published by
Spector Books
Harkortstraße 10
04107 Leipzig
www.spectorbooks.com

Distribution
Germany, Austria: GVA, Gemeinsame Verlagsauslieferung Göttingen GmbH & Co. KG, www.gva-verlage.de
Switzerland: AVA Verlagsauslieferung AG, www.ava.ch
France, Belgium: Interart Paris, www.interart.fr
UK: Central Books Ltd, www.centralbooks.com
USA, Canada, Central and South America, Africa: ARTBOOK/D.A.P., www.artbook.com
South Korea: The Book Society, www.thebooksociety.org
Japan: twelvebooks, www.twelve-books.com
Australia, New Zealand: Perimeter Distribution, www.perimeterdistribution.com

First edition
2024

Printed in the EU

ISBN 978-3-95905-812-4

Supported by
IKOB Museum für Zeitgenössische Kunst / Musée d'Art Contemporain / Museum of Contemporary Art
Phileas The Austrian Office for Contemporary Art
Bundesministerium Kunst, Kultur, öffentlicher Dienst und Sport
Stadt Wien Kultur
Das Land Steiermark → Kultur, Europa, Sport
GRAZ
österreichisches kulturforum bru
ZukunftsFonds der Republik Österreich
Bildrecht
Ostbelgien Mit Unterstützung der Deutschsprachigen Gemeinschaft Belgiens